KETOGENIC MEDITERRANEAN DIET COOKBOOK

Legal Notice

Copyright 2022 Douglas Rand

All rights are reserved.

This book provides information only.

It does not offer health advice.

Consult your doctor before changing your diet.

Ketogenic Mediterranean Diet Cookbook

Ultra Low-Carb Recipes for Heart Health, Weight Loss, and Maximum Longevity

By: Douglas Rand

Contents

Red Meat 15
Beef with Garlic Sauce 16
Air Fryer Pork Chops 17
Steak with Garlic Butter Mushrooms 18
Mediterranean Meatball Lunch Bowls 20
Parma ham Mediterranean plate 21
Italian Meatballs with Mozzarella Cheese 22
Gyro Meat Recipe 23
Lamb Lollipops with Garlic & Rosemary Recipe 25
Low Carb Sloppy Joes 26
Asian Beef Pot Roast 27
Keto Rack of Lamb with Spicy Mint Marmalade 29
Slow Cooker Paleo Pulled Pork 31
Simple Coffee Rubbed Steak 32
Mediterranean Ket Egg Muffins With Ham 33
Taco Casserole 34
Bacon-Wrapped Chipolatas 35
Cheeseburger Casserole 36
Croquettes 37
Slow Roasted Lamb Shoulder 38
Pork Meatballs 39
Tender Beef Cheeks 40

Sweet and Sour Pork 41

Pepper Steak Low Carb Beef Stir Fry 42

Ground Beef and Squash Skillet 43

Keto Schnitzel Crispy Pork 44

Ranch Pork Chops 45

Pork Curry 46

Salami Chips 47

Instant Pot Beef Short Ribs 48

Greek Stuffed Mushrooms 49

Pulled Pork Carnitas 51

Pork and Fennel Soup 53

Pulled Pork Casserole 54

Picadillo Recipe 55

Lamb Korma Curry 56

Sweet Chili Pork Chops 57

5 Spice Pork Tenderloin 58

Lamb Shanks in the Instant Pot 59

Jamaican Jerk Pork Roast 61

Low Carb Beef and Broccoli 62

Poultry 64

Thai Chicken with Basil & Cauliflower Fried Rice 65

Green Chicken Enchilada Cauliflower Casserole 67

Chicken Nugget Meatballs 68

Chicken Cacciatore Meatballs 70

Chicken Salad with Greek Yogurt 72

- Oven-Roasted Za'atar Chicken Breasts 74
- Chicken Pesto Stew with Zoodles 75
- Italian Chicken Parmesan with Cabbage Pasta 76
- Pesto Chicken Casserole With Feta Cheese And Olives 77
- Creamy Tuscan Garlic Chicken 78
- BBQ Chicken Low Carb Healthy Quesadillas 79
- Everything Bagel Chicken Recipe 81
- Chicken Parmesan Casserole 82
- Pistachio Crusted Chicken With Coriander Yogurt Sauce 84
- Chicken Cordon Bleu Meatballs 86
- Thai Chicken Salad 88
- Chicken Tamale Casserole 89
- Chicken & Cauliflower Soup 91
- Peanut Chicken Tenders 92
- Caesar Baked Chicken 93
- Chicken & Chorizo Sheet Pan Dinner 94
- Easy Keto Chicken Shawarma 95
- Belizean Stewed Chicken In The Instant Pot 96
- Chicken Souvlaki With Yogurt Sauce 98
- Instant Pot Turmeric Chicken and Vegetables 99
- Chicken Piccata Meatballs 100
- Asparagus Stuffed Chicken Breast 101
- Crock-Pot Slow Cooker Crack Chicken 102
- Chicken Laksa Recipe 103
- Chicken & Cheese Casserole Bake 104

- Chicken Drumsticks Indonesian Style 105
- Spinach Stuffed Chicken Breast Recipe 106
- Baked Lemon Pepper Wings Recipe 107
- Air Fryer Fried Chicken 108
- Best Garlic Chicken Wings 109
- Roasted Chicken And Vegetables In The Oven 110
- Baked Balsamic Chicken Thighs Recipe 111
- Mexican Cheese And Chicken Stuffed Poblano Peppers 112
- Creamy Dijon Mustard Chicken Recipe 113
- Easy Tandoori Chicken Recipe In The Oven 114
- Seafood 115
- Cod Scrambled Eggs 116
- Crab Cakes 118
- Air Fryer Salmon 119
- Air Fryer Mahi Mahi With Lime Butter 120
- Mediterranean Salmon 121
- 15 Minute Garlic Shrimp Zoodles 122
- Tuna Stuffed Avocado 123
- Mediterranean Tomato Stew With Calamari 124
- Grilled White Fish with Zucchini and Kale Pesto 125
- Superfood Salmon Salad Bowl 126
- Mediterranean Fish Bake 128
- Low Carb Mediterranean Garlic Shrimp 129
- Easy Low Carb Mediterranean Cod 130
- Low Carb Almond Crusted Cod 131

Keto Salmon With Pesto And Spinach 132

Salmon with a Maple Walnut Crusted 133

Roasted Salmon with Parmesan Dill Crust 134

Fattoush salad with Tilapia 135

Spicy Fish Stew 137

Shrimp boil 138

Tuna casserole 139

Baked Salmon with Mayo 140

Keto Mediterranean Battered Fish 141

Creamy Sardine Salad 142

Low carb clam chowder 143

Lemon garlic steam clams 144

Broiled Oyster with Spicy Sauce 145

Crab Stuffed Mushrooms 146

Steamed Clams with Basil Butter 147

Crab legs 148

Low Carb Soft Shell Crab 149

Cajun Trinity Keto Crab Cakes 150

Cheese And Seafood-Stuffed Mushrooms 151

Crabbed Stuffed Avocado with Lime 152

Salmon Meatballs 153

Salmon In Foil Packets With Pesto 154

Ginger Sesame Glazed Salmon 155

Salmon With Garlicky Black Pepper 156

Keto Bacon Wrapped Salmon With Pesto 157

Grilled Salmon With Creamy Pesto Sauce 158

Grilled Salmon Cucumber Salad 159

Cajun Salmon Patties 160

Easy Keto Salmon Cakes 161

Herbed Almond And Parmesan Crusted Fish 162

Baked Lemon Butter Tilapia 163

BLT Lobster Roll Salad 164

Shrimp Cocktail with 3 Sauces 165

Easy Shrimp Scampi 166

Tuna Melts On Tomato Halves 167

Smoky Tuna Pickle Boats 168

Keto Fried Fish 169

Hazelnut Crusted Sea Bass 170

Fantasy Fish Cakes 171

Keto Fish Fingers With Chimichurri Mayo 172

Almond and Parmesan Baked Fish 174

Low-Carb Coconut Fish Curry With Spinach 175

Oven-Baked Fish 176

Low-Carb Cauliflower Sushi 177

Keto Fish Cakes With Roasted Red Pepper 178

Zoodles With Sardines, Tomatoes & Capers 179

Vegetarian Recipes 180

Crispy Air Fryer Brussels sprouts 181

Roasted Air Fryer Cauliflower 182

Cauliflower Tabbouleh 183

Low Carb Mock Cauliflower Potato Salad	184
Parmesan Roasted Ranch Cauliflower With Avocado	185
Instant Pot Green Beans	186
Air Fryer Asparagus	187
Instant Pot Tomato Soup	188
Sautéed Broccolini	189
Keto Cabbage Rolls	190
Mediterranean Cucumber Salad	191
Paleo Low Carb Keto Beef And Broccoli	192
Sandwich Wraps – Sun-dried Tomato & Basil	195
Kale Salad With Goat Cheese And Pomegranate	196
Keto Goat Cheese And Mushroom Frittata	197
Chopped Mediterranean Salad	198
Green Beans and Avocado	199
Feta Cheese Stuffed Bell Peppers	200
Mediterranean Low Carb Broccoli Salad	201
Easy Vegan Cauliflower Fried Rice	202
Mediterranean Collard Green Wraps	203
Spinach Quiche with Crust	204
Garlic Butter Mushrooms	206
Garlic Green Beans with Slivered Almonds	207
Roasted Beetroot & Goat's Cheese Salad	208
Low-Carb Heirloom Tomato Salad Bowl	209
Seafood Salad With Avocado	210
Chicken BLT Salad	211

Warm Kale Salad 212

Keto Cauliflower 'Potato' Salad 213

Salad Sandwiches 215

Wedge Salad 216

French Onion Dip 217

Radish Potato Salad 218

Spinach Ricotta Ravioli 219

Celery Soup 220

Spicy Green Omelet 221

Low Crab Cauliflower Mac Cheese Recipe 222

Latkes 223

Desserts 224

Peanut Butter & Chocolate Pie 225

Low Carb Peanut Butter & Chocolate Truffles 227

Low Carb Thin Mint Macaroon Cookies 228

Pumpkin Spice Haystack Cookies 229

Pistachio Truffles 230

Pistachio Pudding Pie 231

Strawberry Jello Salad 232

Easy Ice Cream Cake 233

Butter Rum Blondies 234

Espresso Chocolate Cheesecake Bars 235

Thumbprint Cookies 236

Keto Mixed Berry Slab Pie 237

Coconut Shortbread Cookies 238

Pistachio Fudge 239
Easy Low Carb Mug Cake 240
Sugar-Free Low Carb Pecan Pie 241
Chocolate Cake 242
Low Carb Pumpkin Cheesecake 243
Low Carb Sugar-Free Blueberry Muffins 244
Lemon Ice Cream 245

Red Meat

Beef with Garlic Sauce

Serves: 4 / Preparation time: 5 minutes / Cooking time: 10 minutes

1 tablespoon cornstarch/tapioca starch

Powdered garlic for garnishing (optional)

2 tablespoons olive oil

1 teaspoon sesame oil

2 teaspoons fresh garlic, minced

1/2 cup sodium-reduced soy sauce

1 lb. flank steak, thinly sliced

- Add oil to a large pan and preheat over medium-high flame.
- Add in garlic and stir-cook for 2 minutes, until golden.
- Toss beef with a tablespoon of cornstarch/tapioca starch and add to a pan with garlic. Cook for about 5 minutes, until browned.
- Next, add in 1 teaspoon sesame oil and 1/2 cup sodium-reduced soy sauce. Cook until sauce begins to thicken.
- Finish with a sprinkle of garlic powder and serve warm!

Air Fryer Pork Chops

Serves: 4 / Preparation time: 5 minutes / Cooking time: 10 minutes

2 teaspoons paprika

1 teaspoon brown sugar/coconut sugar

1 1/4 lbs. bone-in center-cut pork chops (cut 1/2 inch thick)

1 teaspoon garlic powder

1 tablespoon olive oil

1 teaspoon onion powder

1 3/4 teaspoon seasoning salt

1 teaspoon ground mustard

- First, cut large chunks of fat from chops. Rub pork with a tablespoon of olive oil on all sides.
- Add all seasonings to a bowl, mix well and rub into the pork.
- Cook for 5 minutes in your air fryer at 370°F (187 °C).
- Then flip over and continue cooking for another 5 to 6 minutes. The time may vary, depending upon the thickness of the pork.
- The internal temperature of pork should be 145°F (62°C) when done.
- Serve and enjoy your meal!

Steak with Garlic Butter Mushrooms

Serves: 4 / Preparation time: 5 minutes / Cooking time: 20 minutes

4 teaspoons ghee, softened to room temperature

Sea salt

1 lb. grass-fed top sirloin steak (about into 1 1/2 inches thickness)

1 teaspoon fresh garlic, minced

For The Mushrooms:

2 teaspoons ghee, melted

Sea salt

2 cups white mushrooms, thinly sliced

1 teaspoon fresh garlic, minced

- First, preheat your grill over medium-high heat.
- Pat dry steak by using clean paper towels.
- Add a teaspoon of fresh minced garlic to a bowl along with 4 teaspoons ghee and spread half of this mixture all over one side of your steak. Season with salt.
- Place steak onto a preheat grill in a way that butter side remains down and cook until charred, for 4 to 5 minutes.
- Rub remaining mixture over top and flip over the steak. Cook this side too until desired done-ness.
- Once done, remove steak from grill and cover it to keep warm.
- Now add all the ingredients mentioned under the heading of "for the mushrooms" and combine well.
- Take two layers of tinfoil and place on top of one another in a way that shiny side remains inward. Place mushrooms in one layer in center and make a packet by tightly wrapping the side up.
- Place this packet onto a grill in a way that folds of packet facing upward. Grill for about 5 minutes, flip over and continue grilling until mushrooms are tender, for 4 to 5 minutes.
- Once cooked through, serve warm mushrooms over steak and enjoy!

- This keto-Mediterranean meal will make you fall in love and you'll wish to eat it again & again!

Mediterranean Meatball Lunch Bowls

Serves: 5 / Preparation time: 15 minutes / Cooking time: 10 minutes

Meatballs:

Fresh zest from 1 lemon

2 tablespoons ghee or duck fat

500 g ground chicken or turkey

1/4 teaspoon black pepper

1 cup parmesan cheese, grated

1/2 teaspoon sea salt

1 large egg

2 tablespoons any chopped herbs or 2 teaspoons dried Italian herbs

1 clove garlic, minced

Lunch Bowls:

1 small red onion, sliced

5 teaspoons extra virgin olive oil

1 medium cucumber, peeled and sliced

3/4 cup homemade tomato & basil dressing (3 tablespoons per serving)

2-3 regular tomatoes, chopped or 1 1/4 cup cherry tomatoes

1 large head green lettuce such as romaine or butter lettuce

1 large green bell pepper, sliced

- Add all the meatball ingredients in a bowl and mix well. Shape into 25 balls using your hands.
- Grease a large skillet with ghee and preheat over medium-high flame. Once hot, turn the heat down and add in meatballs carefully. Cook until cooked through from inside, each side for 2 to 3 minutes. Once done, remove and set aside.
- Now start folding leaves of lettuce inside Tupperware containers. Add in vegetables.
- Add the meatballs (only 5 balls into each bowl). Drizzle top of each with 3 tablespoons of tomato & basil dressing.
- Drizzle balls with olive oil and serve right away!

Parma ham Mediterranean plate

Serves: 1 / Preparation time: 25 minutes / Cooking time: 0 minutes

2 cherry tomatoes, sliced in half

3 oz. prosciutto

1 teaspoon fresh lemons juice

4 tablespoons mixed leafy greens

1 large egg, boiled

½ oz. scallions, thinly sliced

2 oz. avocados, sliced

3 tablespoons feta cheese, crumbled

Salt and pepper, to taste

1 teaspoon fresh lemons juice

1 tablespoon olive oil

- Lay a bed of lettuce onto a plate and add all the ingredients listed above except for last 3 ingredients.
- Finish with a drizzle of olive oil, lemon juice, and sprinkle with pepper and salt, to your preference.

Italian Meatballs with Mozzarella Cheese

Serves: 4 / Preparation time: 20 minutes / Cooking time: 30 minutes

Salt and pepper, to taste

1 lb. ground beef or ground turkey

5 oz. fresh mozzarella cheese, cut into bite-sized pieces

2 oz. parmesan cheese, shredded (¾ cup)

2 oz. butter

1 egg

7 oz. fresh spinach (6½ cups)

½ teaspoon ground black pepper

1 teaspoon salt

2 tablespoons fresh parsley, finely chopped

½ tablespoon dried basil

1¾ cups canned whole tomatoes

½ teaspoon onion powder

3 tablespoons olive oil

1 teaspoon garlic powder

- Add parmesan cheese to a bowl along with spices, salt, egg, and ground beef. Blend thoroughly. Shape into meatballs (30 grams each). Make sure to keep your hands wet while shaping the balls.
- Add olive oil to a large skillet and preheat over medium-high heat. Add in meatballs and cook until golden on all sides.
- Turn the heat down and add in canned tomatoes. Simmer for approximately 15 minutes, stirring every few minutes.
- Add in pepper and salt, to taste. Stir in 2 tablespoons of finely chopped parsley.
- Add butter to a separate pan and let it melt. Then add in spinach and cook for a minute or two, stirring frequently. Season with pepper and salt, to your preference.
- Add sautéed spinach to meatballs and stir until combined.
- Top with mozzarella cheese and serve this delicious keto-Mediterranean meal immediately!

Gyro Meat Recipe

Serves: 8 / Preparation time: 15 minutes / Cooking time: 50 minutes

2 teaspoons dried marjoram

1/2 teaspoon black pepper

1 medium onion, cut into chunks

2 teaspoons sea salt

4 cloves garlic

1 teaspoon cumin

1 lb. ground lamb

2 teaspoons dried rosemary

1 lb. ground beef

2 teaspoons dried thyme

1 tablespoon dried oregano

- Preheat your oven to a temperature of 300°F (148°C).
- Take a loaf pan (9x5) and line it with foil or parchment paper.
- Puree onion and garlic in a food processor, scraping the sides of processor with spatula.
- Transfer this mixture to a clean kitchen rowel, twist both the ends, and squeeze as much as possible to release liquid (about 1/2 cup).
- Discard this mixture and transfer dried onion-garlic mixture back to a food processor.
- Add in 1/2 teaspoon black pepper, herbs, 1 lb. ground lamb, and 1 lb. ground beef. Continue processing for a minute or two, until texture resembles a paste, scraping down the sides, as needed.
- Add this mixture to a prepared lined pan, pressing down as much as possible.
- Bake until an internal temperature reaches to 165°F (73°C). It will take around 45 to 55 minutes.
- Once done, take out from oven and drain the fat.
- Cover with foil until temperature reaches 175°F (79°C).
- Remove from pan and allow to cool. Refrigerate until chilled, for 2 to 3 hours at least.
- Thinly slice the meatloaf.

- Preheat a nonstick skillet (grease with a little oil, if desired).
- Add gyro meat in a pan in a single layer and cook each side for 2 to 3 minutes, until browned. Do this in batches.
- Serve delicious and taste gyro meat slices with your favorite toppings.

Lamb Lollipops with Garlic & Rosemary Recipe

Serves: 2 / Preparation time: 10 minutes / Cooking time: 10 minutes

2–3 tablespoons olive oil

Salt and pepper, to taste

8 lamb lollipops

2–3 fresh rosemary sprigs, removed from sprig

2 garlic cloves, minced

- Season both sides of lamb with generous amount of pepper and salt.
- Sprinkle each side with a little rosemary, pressing down a bit.
- Add oil to a large cast iron skillet and preheat over medium-high flame.
- Add in sprig of rosemary (about 2 tablespoons removed from stem) and garlic and spread evenly.
- Add in lamb and sear each side for 4 to 5 minutes.
- Garnish with fresh rosemary and enjoy!

Low Carb Sloppy Joes

Serves: 4 / Preparation time: 5 minutes / Cooking time: 20 minutes

1 teaspoon red wine vinegar

Parsley, chopped, for garnish (optional)

1/2 tablespoon olive oil

Cheese, for garnish (optional)

1/3 cup green onions, thinly sliced

Lettuce, for serving

1 lb. ground beef (85%)

Pinch of black pepper

3/4 cup tomato sauce, canned

Pinch of crushed red pepper flakes

1/2 cup low-sodium beef bone broth or low-sodium beef broth

1/2 teaspoon prepared yellow mustard

1 1/2 tablespoons tomato paste

1/2 teaspoon sea salt

1 tablespoon monkfruit sweetener, or granulated sugar

1 teaspoon chili powder

1 tablespoon Worcestershire sauce

- Preheat olive oil in a frying pan. Add in green onions and cook for 60 seconds.
- Next, add in beef and continue cooking until beef is no longer pink, for about 5 minutes, breaking it up as possible.
- Whisk together remaining ingredients and pour into the pan with cooked beef. Bring everything to a boil.
- Once begins to boil. Turn the heat down and simmer for about 9 to 10 minutes, until sauce has thickened.
- Spoon this gravy over lettuce followed by cheese and parsley on top.
- It's ready to serve!

Asian Beef Pot Roast

Serves: Twelve 4 oz. servings / Preparation time: 10 minutes / Cooking time: 40 minutes

For The Pot Roast:

2 tablespoons granulated sugar substitute

1 teaspoon red wine vinegar

1 boneless chuck roast

1 tablespoon granulated sugar substitute

3 cloves garlic, crushed

1 tablespoon orange zest

2 tablespoons fresh ginger, peeled and chopped

1/2 cup water

1 teaspoon orange extract

1 teaspoon crushed red pepper flakes

1/4 cup sugar free fish sauce

Recommended Garnish Options:

Chopped cilantro

Chopped scallions

Shredded red cabbage

Fresh orange zest

Butter lettuce leaves

For The Sriracha Orange Sauce:

1 teaspoon Sriracha hot sauce

1/2 teaspoon fresh orange zest

1/4 cup sugar free mayonnaise

1 teaspoon granulated sugar substitut

- For the pot roast: For Add whole chuck roast to your Instant pot along with 1/4 cup sugar free fish sauce, 3 crushed cloves of garlic, 1 teaspoon crushed red pepper flakes, 1 teaspoon orange extract , 2 tablespoons freshly chopped ginger, 1/2 cup water, and 2 tablespoons granulated sugar substitute. Mix well.
- Put on the lid of your Instant Pot and turn on the setting of "Manual." Cook on "High" for 35 minutes.
- Once cycle has completed, release pressure according to the manufacturer's directions.
- Remove lid and stir in a tablespoon of sweetener, 1 teaspoon red wine vinegar, and 1 tablespoon orange zest.
- Cook for 5 minutes on "Sauté" mode.

- Turn off the heat and shred the meat.
- Serve in a bowl or lettuce leaves along with your favorite garnishes.
- For the Sriracha sauce: Add all the sauce ingredients in a bowl and mix well.

Keto Rack of Lamb with Spicy Mint Marmalade

Serves: 4 / Preparation time: 10 minutes / Cooking time: 25 minutes

2 tablespoons olive oil

1/4 teaspoon ground black pepper

2 racks of lamb (8 ribs each)

1/2 teaspoon kosher salt

For The Spice Coating:

1 tablespoon olive oil

1/4 teaspoon garlic powder

1 teaspoon balsamic vinegar

1/2 teaspoon dried rosemary

1 teaspoon Dijon mustard

1/4 teaspoon fennel seeds, chopped or crushed

For the Spicy Mint Marmalade:

1/2 teaspoon red pepper flakes

2 teaspoons lime juice

1/4 cup sugar free orange marmalade

2 teaspoons unsweetened fish sauce

1/2 cup fresh mint leaves

2 tablespoons avocado oil

- Preheat your oven to 450° F (230° C).
- Add 2 tablespoons of oil to a cast iron skillet and preheat over medium-high flame.
- Season the lamb with pepper and salt on all sides.
- Sear each side of lamb for approx. 2 minutes, and then remove from skillet.
- Add all the spice coating ingredients in a separate bowl and mix well.
- Brush lamb with spice coating mixture on all sides.
- Place lamb in a roasting pan in a way that fat side remains up.
- Roast until your desired internal temperature is reached, 10 minutes for rare.
- Remember that lamb will continue cooking after removing from heat. So make sure to keep it out a few degrees under your desired temperature.
- Once done, cover with foil loosely and let it leave for 10 minutes.
- Once cooled enough, cut and serve warm!

- For Marmalade: Blend together all the marmalade ingredients in a blender, until smooth.
- Chill until ready to serve!

Slow Cooker Paleo Pulled Pork

Serves: 8 / Preparation time: 10 minutes / Cooking time: 8 hours

Fresh cilantro

1 tablespoon onion powder

Paleo friendly BBQ sauce

1 tablespoon garlic powder

8-10 Whole wheat OR Gluten free hamburger buns (You can go for lettuce for paleo option)

2 teaspoons grated fresh ginger

1 bay leaf

1/2 teaspoon cumin

1 1/2 teaspoons ground cloves

1 cup apple cider or apple juice

1 1/2 teaspoons ground allspice

3 lbs. boneless pork butt

1 1/2 teaspoons thyme

1/4 teaspoon cayenne pepper

1 1/2 teaspoons dry mustard

1/4 teaspoon black pepper

1 1/2 teaspoons coarse salt

1/2 teaspoon sugar

1 teaspoon sweet or hot paprika

- Add all the ingredients in bowl except for apple juice/apple cider and pork butt. Whisk well.
- Rub spices together with your fingers to ensure they everything is evenly dispersed. Rub pork with this mixture on all sides.
- Place pork in a slow cooker in a way that fat side remains up followed by apple juice/vinegar over top.
- Add in bay leaf and cook for 8 hours on low.
- Once done, Remove and shred pork with the help of forks
- Skim off the fat from the liquid in cooker and drizzle this liquid over meat (a couple of tablespoons). Stir around and serve on a lettuce or on a bun with BBQ sauce.
- Finish with a sprinkle of fresh cilantro!

Simple Coffee Rubbed Steak

Serves: 2 / Preparation time: 10 minutes / Cooking time: 10 minutes

1/2 teaspoon smoked paprika

1/2 lb. New York strip steak

1 teaspoon ground coffee

2 tablespoons unsweetened coconut flakes, for garnishing

1/4 teaspoon salt

Pinch of pepper

1/4 teaspoon garlic powder

1/8 teaspoon cinnamon

1/4 teaspoon onion powder

1 teaspoon coconut sugar

1/2 teaspoon chili powder

1 teaspoon unsweetened cocoa powder

- Add all the rub ingredients in a bowl and mix well.
- Cut visible, large fat chunks off the steak. Coat steal with rub mix on all sides.
- Cover and place in a refrigerator for an hour
- Spray a regular or grill pan with cooking spray and preheat over high.
- Preheat your oven to 400° F (200°C).
- Cook each side of steak for a minute or two, until nicely seared.
- Turn the heat down and cook until it has cooked through.
- Once done, remove steak to a platter and cover with foil.
- In the meantime, add coconut flakes on a baking tray lined with parchment paper and toast for just a minute or two.
- Top steak with toasted coconut flakes and enjoy warm!

Mediterranean Ket Egg Muffins With Ham

Serves: 6 / Preparation time: 10 minutes / Cooking time: 15 minutes

5 large eggs

Fresh basil for garnish

9 slices of thin cut deli ham

1 1/2 tablespoons pesto sauce

1/2 cup canned roasted red pepper, sliced plus more for garnish

Pinch of pepper

1/3 cup fresh spinach, minced

Pinch of salt

1/4 cup feta cheese, crumbled

- Preheat your oven to 400 degrees F (200 degrees C).
- Spray a muffin tin generously with cooking spray.
- Line each muffin with 1.5 pieces of ham. Do not leave any holes otherwise egg mixture will explode out.
- Place a bit of roasted red pepper in each tin at bottom followed a tablespoon of minced spinach on top of each.
- Top with half heaping tablespoon of crumbled feta cheese.
- Add eggs to a separate bowl and whisk with pepper and salt. Divide this mixture among each muffin tin equally.
- Bake until eggs are set and puffy. This will take 15 to 17 minutes.
- Garnish each cup with 1/4 teaspoon of pesto sauce after removing from tin.
- Finish with a garnish of fresh basil and slices of roasted red pepper.

Taco Casserole

Serves: 4 / Preparation time: 5 minutes / Cooking time: 25 minutes

Salt, to taste

4 tablespoons sour cream

7 oz. basic ground beef

2 tablespoons tomato, diced

1 teaspoon garlic powder

¼ cup black olives, sliced

2 teaspoons taco seasoning

1 scallion, sliced

4 large eggs

Pepper, to taste

1 cup cheddar cheese, shredded

- First, preheat your oven to a temperature of 350° F (176°C).
- Mix together beef, 2 teaspoons taco seasoning, and 1 teaspoon garlic powder in a medium-sized bowl.
- Add in beaten eggs and stir well.
- Add in half of the cheese along with pepper and salt to taste.
- Add beef mixture to a greased casserole dish and top with remaining cheese.
- Bake in the oven for 20-25 minutes.
- Once done, take it out and garnish it with olives, scallions, and tomato.
- Slice into 4 pieces and serve warm with a dollop of sour cream.
- Wow! Too yummy!

Bacon-Wrapped Chipolatas

Serves: 8 / Preparation time: 5 minutes / Cooking time: 30 minutes

16 beef or pork chipolata sausages

16 slices bacon

⅓ cup keto barbecue sauce

- First, preheat your oven to a temperature of 400°F (204°C).
- Wrap sausages in a bacon slice, securing with a toothpick.
- Place in a roasting tray and roast in a preheated oven for 10 minutes.
- Then take it out from the oven and brush with half of the keto BBQ sauce.
- Continue roasting for another 10 minutes, brush with sauce, and continue cooking until sausages are cooked through, for 10 to 15 minutes.
- Take the dish out of the oven and cool for a few minutes.
- Remove the toothpicks carefully and serve warm!

Cheeseburger Casserole

Serves: 6 / Preparation time: 10 minutes / Cooking time: 40 minutes

¼ cup sugar-free tomato ketchup

1/4 cup heavy cream

1 teaspoon olive oil

3 large eggs

1 lb. ground beef

1 cup cheddar cheese, shredded

½ teaspoon salt

1 teaspoon garlic powder

¼ teaspoon white pepper ground

2 tablespoons Worcestershire sauce

5 oz. bacon, diced

¼ cup low carb mayonnaise

1 small onion, diced

¼ cup yellow mustard

2 dill pickles, sliced

- First, preheat your oven to 375°F (190°C).
- Preheat oil in a large saucepan and add in ground beef along with pepper and salt. Cook until beef is browned, breaking it up. Once done, turn the flame off.
- To a nonstick frying pan, add bacon and sauté over medium-high flame until crisp, draining off the fat.
- Once cooked through, add bacon to a beef mixture along with half the cheddar cheese, ¼ cup low carb mayonnaise, 1 teaspoon garlic powder, 2 tablespoons Worcestershire sauce, ¼ cup tomato ketchup, sliced pickles, ¼ cup yellow mustard, and diced onion. Mix everything well and add to a casserole dish.
- In a separate bowl, combine together 1/4 cup heavy cream and 3 large eggs and pour over beef mixture.
- Sprinkle top with remaining cheese and bake in a preheated oven for half an hour.

Croquettes

Serves: 14 Croquettes / Preparation time: 10 minutes / Cooking time: 20 minutes

1 egg	2 teaspoons pepper
1 tablespoon almond meal	3 slices bacon, diced into small pieces
1 lb. broccoli	1 teaspoon salt
1 tablespoon flaxseed ground	1/2 cup parmesan, grated
2 oz. butter	2 oz. pork rinds, crushed into crumbs

- Steam/boil broccoli until tender for about 5 minutes, then drain well.
- Blend butter and warm broccoli together until you have a puree. Add to w bowl and stir in pepper, salt, and parmesan.
- Sauté bacon pieces for 6 to 8 minutes, over medium heat. Once done, add bacon and its fat to a bowl with broccoli. Combine well.
- Chill this mixture for half an hour.
- After 30 minutes, preheat your deep fryer to 350°F (176 °C).
- Add pork rinds and egg to the beef mixture and mix well. Roll into barrel shapes (at least 14).
- Combine together a tablespoon of each almond meal and flaxseed meal on a plate.
- Now start rolling croquettes, one by one, into the meal mix until coated on all sides, pressing lightly with your hands.
- Deep fry the croquettes in hot oil for 3 to 6 minutes, until golden brown and crisp. Do this in batches.
- Serve and enjoy!

Slow Roasted Lamb Shoulder

Serves: 10 / Preparation time: 10 minutes / Cooking time: 5-6hours

- 2 teaspoon cumin ground
- 4 lbs. lamb shoulder bone-in
- 3 tablespoons olive oil
- 1 lemon, zest, and juice
- 4 cloves garlic, crushed
- ½ teaspoon chili powder
- 1 tablespoon dried mint
- 1 teaspoon salt
- 2 teaspoons cinnamon ground

- Add all the ingredients to a small-sized bowl except for lamb and combine well.
- Cut deep scores on the lamb shoulder all over and rub with the marinade.
- Marinate overnight or for 4 hours at least.
- After marinating, preheat your oven to a temperature of 300°F (148°C).
- Cook lamb in a large roasting tin for 5-5 ½ hours. Cover with aluminum foil after the first hour of cooking.
- Once done, take it out of the oven and leave for 15 to 20 minutes.
- Slice and enjoy with cauliflower mash and keto gravy.

Pork Meatballs

Serves: 8 / Preparation time: 15 minutes / Cooking time: 25 minutes

1 tablespoon apple cider vinegar

1 teaspoon pepper

2 pounds ground pork

1 teaspoon salt

7 oz. cheddar cheese, shredded

1 egg

2 tablespoons Dijon mustard

3 tablespoons sage fresh, finely chopped

2 tablespoons sugar-free maple syrup

2 cloves garlic, crushed

- Add all the ingredients to a large-sized bowl and mix well.
- Shape into balls (2 tablespoons each).
- Preheat the oven to 390°F (198°C).
- Place meatballs onto a roasting tray lined with parchment.
- Bake in a preheated oven until golden, for 20 to 25 minutes.
- Once done, remove, serve & enjoy!

Tender Beef Cheeks

Serves: 4 / Preparation time: 5 minutes / Cooking time: 8 hours

1 cup tamari sauce

2 lbs. beef cheeks 4 pieces

1 orange zest only

1 cinnamon stick

2 scallions, cut into 1-in. lengths

3-star anise

3 cloves garlic, sliced

1 tablespoon sesame oil

2 in fresh ginger, sliced

1/3 cup sukrin gold

1/2 cup Chinese cooking wine

- Add lemon zest to a slow cooker along with remaining ingredients except for beef cheeks.
- Once sweetener has dissolved, add in beef cheeks and stir until coated with sauce.
- Cook for 8 hours on low.
- Once cooked through, serve delicious Mediterranean beef cheeks with cauliflower rice and a little cooking broth.

Sweet and Sour Pork

Serves: 4 / Preparation time: 20 minutes / Cooking time: 20 minutes

1 lb. pork butt, sliced into strips

2 teaspoons sesame seeds

1/3 cup almond flour

2 scallions, thinly sliced

2 tablespoons unflavored protein powder (low carb)

1 recipe Keto Sweet and Sour Sauce

1 teaspoon baking powder

1/4 cup red pepper, diced

Pinch salt

1/4 cup green pepper, diced

1 large egg

2 teaspoons sesame oil

2-3 tablespoons sparkling water chilled

- Preheat your deep fryer 355° F (179°C).
- Combine together 2 tablespoons protein powder, 1/3 cup almond flour, pinch of salt, and 1 teaspoon baking powder in a small-sized bowl.
- Add in sparkling water and eggs and continue whisking until you have a thick batter.
- Dip pork strips into the prepared batter and drops into hot oil gently, flipping in between using tongs. Do this in batches, if needed.
- Once cooked through, remove to an absorbent paper and leave until drained.
- Add oil to a nonstick frying pan and sauté pepper for 5 to 8 minutes over high heat.
- Then turn the heat down and stir in keto sweet and sour sauce until warmed through.
- Deep fry pork strips until golden brown and drains again.
- Add pork strips to a sauce and toss until coated.
- Sprinkle with sesame seeds and scallions.
- Bon appetite!

Pepper Steak Low Carb Beef Stir Fry

Serves: 4 / Preparation time: 10 minutes / Cooking time: 10 minutes

¼ cup onion, chopped

15 oz. baby corn (optional)

1 tablespoon sesame oil or avocado oil

¼ teaspoon xanthan gum + additional if needed (optional thickener)

1 lb. thin sticks of sirloin steak

8 oz. mushrooms, sliced

1 clove garlic, minced

2 tablespoon soy sauce or tamari

Salt and pepper, to taste

½ cup beef broth

1 medium green bell pepper, cut into strips

- Preheat oil in a large skillet and add in beef strips and garlic. Cook well until beef is browned on all sides.
- When cooked thoroughly, season with pepper and salt to your preferences.
- Turn off the flame and remove it to a plate.
- Add a little bit of oil to the same pan and cook onion and pepper until tender.
- Next, add in the remaining ingredients and continue cooking until mushrooms are softened.
- Stir in beef trips and cook until warmed through.
- Enjoy!

Ground Beef and Squash Skillet

Serves: 4 / Preparation time: 10 minutes / Cooking time: 20 minutes

1 tablespoon soy sauce

1 lb. ground beef

1 medium green bell pepper, chopped

1 tablespoon garlic, minced

1 medium tomato, chopped

1 teaspoon dried minced onion

1 medium summer squash yellow or green

Dash salt, or to taste

Dash pepper, or to taste

Dash of pepper, or to taste

- Add hamburger to a skillet and brown with onion, garlic, pepper, and salt.
- Next, add in soy sauce, chopped bell pepper, tomato, and squash.
- Mix well and cook until veggies are tender, for about 20 minutes on low.
- It's ready!

Keto Schnitzel Crispy Pork

Serves: 4 / Preparation time: 10 minutes / Cooking time: 10 minutes

1 tablespoon water

Peanut oil, sufficient for your deep fryer

14 oz. pork top round, cut into 4 thin steaks

1/2 teaspoon pepper

1 egg

1 tablespoon Italian herb & spice blend

1 tablespoon heavy cream

3/4 cup parmesan cheese, finely grated

- Preheat your deep fryer to a temperature of 355° F (179°C).
- Pound the pork steaks to a thickness of 1/4in/0.5cm by rolling pin or meat mallet.
- Combine together 1 tablespoon heavy cream, egg, and 1 tablespoon water until combined.
- Mix together 1 tablespoon Italian herb & spice blend, 3/4 cup grated parmesan cheese, and 1/2 teaspoon pepper in a small tray.
- Dip each pork steak first into an egg mixture and then coat with cheese mixture, pressing it into the steak.
- Place schnitzels inside a preheated deep fryer and cook for 5 to 7 minutes, until cooked through. Do this in batches, if needed.
- Once done, remove to a towel-lined plate and drain well before serving.

Ranch Pork Chops

Serves: 4 / Preparation time: 10 minutes / Cooking time: 20 minutes

3 tablespoons keto ranch spice mix

Fresh parsley, to serve

1 lb. green beans, trimmed

4 (7 oz.) pork chops bone-in

1 pound radishes halved

Pepper, to taste

2 tablespoons olive oil

Salt, to taste

2 cloves garlic, finely chopped

- Preheat your oven to a temperature of 390°F (198°C).
- Add beans to a large mixing bowl along with half the ranch spice mix, oil, radishes, garlic, and a generous pinch of pepper and salt. Mix well.
- Spread this mixture onto a large-sized sheet pan, leaving spaces for pork chops.
- Place chops into spaces and sprinkle with a pinch of pepper, salt, and remaining ranch spice.
- Roast in the oven until pork chops are cooked through, for 15 to 20 minutes.
- Once done, broil the chops for a few minutes until browned.
- Finish with a sprinkle of parsley and enjoy!

Pork Curry

Serves: 6 / Preparation time: 10 minutes / Cooking time: 1 hour 10 minutes

1 medium onion, diced

1/2 lb. green beans, sliced into 2-inch lengths

2 lbs. pork butt

1/2 teaspoon salt

1 teaspoon cumin ground

1 lime zest and juice

1 teaspoon coriander ground

14 oz. coconut cream

1/2 teaspoon cinnamon ground

1-inch ginger, finely sliced

1/2 teaspoon chili powder

3 cloves garlic, crushed

2 tablespoons coconut oil

- Combine together 1/2 teaspoon chili powder, 1 teaspoon coriander ground, 1 teaspoon cumin ground, and 1/2 teaspoon cinnamon ground in a medium-sized bowl. Add in diced pork and mix until coated with spices. Marinate overnight or for 2 hours at least.
- Preheat coconut oil in a large saucepan and sauté finely sliced ginger, 3 crushed cloves of garlic, and diced onion for 5 minutes.
- Add in marinated pork and cook until evenly colored, for 5 to 7 minutes.
- Pour over 14 oz. Coconut cream and bring everything to a simmer.
- Simmer until pork is tender for 60 to 80 minutes.
- Next, stir in green beans, lime juice, and salt for 5 minutes.
- Serve warm!

Salami Chips

Serves: 4 / Preparation time: 10 minutes / Cooking time: 8 hours

1/3 cup franks hot sauce

10 oz. salami, thinly sliced

- Add hot sauce to a bowl and coat each slice of salami with it, dripping off excess.
- Place coated salami pieces on food dehydrator trays and stack them onto their base.
- Put on its lid and set it to high.
- Dehydrate for 8 to 10 hours. Time may vary, so keep an eye on it.
- Once dried completely, remove to a serving bowl and serve with any delicious low-carb dip.

Instant Pot Beef Short Ribs

Serves: 8 / Preparation time: 5 minutes / Cooking time: 45 minutes

4 cloves garlic, sliced

1 cup beef stock

8 beef short ribs bone-in

1 teaspoon salt

3 tablespoons olive oil

1 teaspoon dried thyme

1 small onion, diced

- Preheat a tablespoon of oil in a large frying pan.
- Once hot, add in ribs and cook on all sides until browned. Remove and set aside.
- Turn on the setting of your Instant Pot to Sauté mode.
- Add in remaining oil, salt, thyme, sliced garlic, and diced. Sauté everything until onions have softened, for 5 minutes.
- Stir in 1 cup beef stock and cook short ribs.
- Secure the lid of your pot and cook for 30 minutes on high pressure. For large ribs, the cooking time will be 45 minutes.
- Once the timer goes off, release the steam via the natural method and then remove the lid carefully.
- Remove ribs into a lined roasting tray.
- Pour half of the pot liquid into a small saucepan and bring to a boil until reduced by half. After that, use an immersion blender to smooth.
- Broil ribs until crispy for 5 minutes.
- Drizzle ribs with sauce and enjoy with coleslaw.

Greek Stuffed Mushrooms

Serves: 3 / Preparation time: 15 minutes / Cooking time: 25 minutes

7 oz. basic ground beef

Pepper, to taste

6 portobello mushrooms, stalks removed

Salt, to taste

1 tablespoon olive oil

½ cup feta cheese, diced

½ red onion, diced

¼ cup kalamata olives, chopped

1 teaspoon garlic powder

1 tablespoon red wine vinegar

1 teaspoon dried oregano

1 cup baby spinach, roughly chopped

½ teaspoon dried mint

1 small tomato, diced

- Preheat the oven to 375° F (190°C).
- Take a baking sheet and line it with parchment.
- Place mushrooms onto a prepared baking sheet.
- Spray both sides of mushrooms with oil and then season with pepper and salt.
- Bake in a preheated oven until cooked through, for 10 to 12 minutes, pouring off any excess liquid.
- Meanwhile, preheat oil in a nonstick frying pan and sauté onion for 3 minutes.
- Stir in 1 teaspoon dried oregano, 1 teaspoon garlic powder, and ½ teaspoon dried mint.
- Next, add in cooked ground beef.
- Add in diced tomato and continue cooking for 2 minutes.
- Stir in a cup of roughly chopped spinach, ¼ cup chopped olives, and 1 tablespoon red wine vinegar and cook for a minute.
- Sprinkle over ½ cup of diced feta cheese and turn off the flame. Keep the pan aside until mushrooms are cooked.
- Remove excess liquid from mushrooms using a clean paper towel.

- Spoon the meat mixture over mushrooms and cook for 5 to 10 minutes in an oven, or until cheese has slightly brown on top.
- Wow! Looks amazing!

Pulled Pork Carnitas

Serves: 12 / Preparation time: 10 minutes / Cooking time: 2 hours 10 minutes

2 tablespoons olive oil

2 cups chicken stock

5 lbs. pork shoulder (butt) boneless, any string or netting removed

2 limes, zest, and juice

2 tablespoons erythritol

4 cloves garlic, crushed

1 teaspoon dried oregano

2 large jalapenos, sliced

1 teaspoon salt

1 small onion, diced

1 teaspoon pepper

1/4 cup salted butter

- Unroll pork and cut deep slits for even marinating.
- Brush pork with olive oil on both sides and then season with 1 teaspoon salt, 1 teaspoon dried oregano, 1 teaspoon pepper, and 2 tablespoons erythritol. Marinate overnight or for 3 hours at least.
- Turn on the setting of your Instant Pot to Sauté and add in sliced jalapenos, diced onion, crushed garlic, and 1/4 cup salted butter. Sauté until onion turns translucent, stirring in between.
- Next, add in 2 cups chicken stock, lime zest, lime juice, and then marinated pork (skin and fat should be on top).
- Secure the lid of your Instant Pot and cook for 2 hours on high pressure.
- Once the timer goes off, release the pressure naturally and remove the lid carefully.
- Remove pork using tongs to a baking tray and shred with forks.
- Turn on the heat to high again and cook until juice is reduced to 2 cups only.
- Pour these juices over shredded pork.
- Preheat a tablespoon of oil in a nonstick pan and add in pork, pressing down gently.

- Cook until you get your desired crispness.

Pork and Fennel Soup

Serves: 6 / Preparation time: 10 minutes / Cooking time: 6 hours

1 teaspoon salt

1 cup heavy cream

1 lb. pork butt

2 cups chicken stock

1 lb. cauliflower, cut into florets

2 cups water

10 oz. fresh fennel, sliced

½ teaspoon white pepper ground

2 cloves garlic, quartered

- Add all the ingredients to a slow cooker except for cream and cook for 6 hours on high.
- Remove pork and shred it using forks. Keep it aside.
- Puree soup using an immersion blender until you have smooth consistency.
- Stir in shredded pork and a cup of heavy cream.
- Adjust pepper and salt, if desired.
- Serve right away!

Pulled Pork Casserole

Serves: 4 / Preparation time: 15 minutes / Cooking time: 20 minutes

2 cups cauliflower riced

1/4 cup scallions, sliced

2 tablespoons butter

1 medium tomato, diced

1 clove garlic, crushed

1 cup cheddar cheese, grated

1 small green pepper, diced

2 tablespoons cilantro, chopped

1 medium zucchini, diced

2 serves low carb enchilada sauce

1/2 teaspoon pepper ground

2 tablespoons lime juice

1/4 teaspoon salt

6 oz. low carb pork carnitas

- Add 2 tablespoons butter to a large pan along with crushed garlic and diced green pepper. Sauté for 5 minutes.
- Then add in 1/4 teaspoon salt, 1/2 teaspoon pepper ground, and diced zucchini and continue sautéing for another 5 minutes.
- Next, add in 2 cups of cauliflower riced and stir-cook for 5 more minutes.
- Add in 2 tablespoons lime juice and carnitas and stir well.
- Stir in enchilada sauce and bring everything to a simmer.
- Sprinkle with cheese and cilantro after cooking for 5 minutes and turn the stove off. Broil for 2 to 3 minutes, until cheese has melted.
- Finish with a garnish of sliced scallions and diced tomato.
- Serve immediately!

Picadillo Recipe

Serves: 7 / Preparation time: 10 minutes / Cooking time: 25 minutes

1 teaspoon coriander ground

1/2 cup cilantro, chopped

2 tablespoons olive oil

5 oz. green olives, pitted and sliced

1 onion, diced

1 green pepper, deseeded and diced

3 cloves of garlic, minced

1 1/2 cups tomato passata

1 teaspoon salt

1/2 cup beef stock

1/2 teaspoon pepper

1 pinch saffron

2 tablespoons cumin seeds

1 teaspoon erythritol

2 teaspoons dried oregano leaves

1 teaspoon smoked paprika ground

1 teaspoon garlic powder

- Preheat oil in a large saucepan and add in 3 minced cloves of garlic, diced onion, 1/2 teaspoon pepper, and 1 teaspoon salt. Sauté for 5 minutes.
- Next, add in 2 tablespoons cumin seeds, 1 teaspoon garlic powder, 2 teaspoons dried oregano leaves, 1 teaspoon erythritol, 1 teaspoon coriander ground, 1 teaspoon smoked paprika ground, and 1 pinch of saffron. Sauté for 3 minutes and then add in ground beef. Cook until beef is browned on all sides.
- Add in 1 1/2 cups tomato passata and 1/2 cup beef stock and continue simmering until the sauce has thickened, for 15 to 20 minutes.
- Add in half the cilantro, pitted and sliced olives, and diced green pepper. Stir well and cook for 5 minutes.
- Top picadillo with remaining cilantro and serve with cauliflower rice.

Lamb Korma Curry

Serves: 15 / Preparation time: 15 minutes / Cooking time: 2 hours

1 1/2 tablespoons coriander ground

11 oz. full-fat Greek yogurt

4 lbs. lamb shoulder, cut into a large dice

1 teaspoon white pepper

1-inch ginger

1-2 teaspoons salt

6 cloves garlic

1 cup water

1 small onion

1 cup heavy cream

3 oz. ghee

2 teaspoons turmeric ground

1 cinnamon stick

2 teaspoons Kashmiri chili powder

2 tablespoons garam masala

1 1/2 tablespoon cumin ground

1 1/2 tablespoons ginger ground

- Add onion to a food processor and ginger and garlic and blend until chopped finely.
- Mix together all the spices in a small-sized bowl and set it aside.
- Preheat ghee in a large saucepan and add in onion-garlic mixture along with a cinnamon stick. Sauté until begins to caramelize, for 10 to 15 minutes over low flame.
- Raise the heat and add in diced lamb. Cook until browned.
- Next, stir in spice mixture until lamb is coated completely.
- Add in 1 cup water and 1 cup heavy cream, stir well and bring to a simmer.
- Drop down the heat and partially cover the pan. Simmer for 2 hours, stirring occasionally. If the sauce seems too much thick, you can add half a cup of water.
- Add 11 oz. full-fat Greek yogurt, 1 teaspoon white pepper, and 1-2 teaspoons salt.
- Stir well and continue simmering for another 10 minutes.
- Turn off the flame and remove it to a serving platter.
- Serve delicious lamb korma curry with cauliflower rice.

Sweet Chili Pork Chops

Serves: 4 / Preparation time: 10 minutes / Cooking time: 10 minutes

4 pork chops (6 oz. each)

1/4 teaspoon ground black pepper

1 tablespoon avocado oil

1/2 teaspoon kosher salt

For The Sauce:

1/2 teaspoon sesame oil

3 tablespoons scallions, chopped + additional for garnish

3 tablespoons sugar-free orange marmalade

1/4 teaspoon habanero peppers, chopped

1 teaspoon lime juice

1/4 teaspoon dried red pepper flakes

1 teaspoon fish sauce

- Preheat oil in a large skillet.
- Season the pork chops with pepper and salt on all sides.
- Cook each side for 3 to 4 minutes, or until completely cooked through.
- Once done, remove to a serving platter.
- To the same pan, add all the sauce ingredients and stir well.
- Cook until sauce has thickened, for 2 to 3 minutes.
- Pour over cooked pork chops.
- Serve warm!

5 Spice Pork Tenderloin

Serves: 10 / Preparation time: 5 minutes / Cooking time: 20 minutes

For The Tenderloin:

3 lbs. pork tenderloin

2 teaspoons red chilis, chopped (for garnish)

1 tablespoon + 1 teaspoon 5 spice powder

2 tablespoons scallions, chopped (for garnish)

1 tablespoon granulated erythritol sweetener

1 tablespoon avocado oil

1 teaspoon kosher salt

For The Sauce:

2 teaspoons ginger, minced

2 teaspoons sesame oil

2 tablespoons lime juice

2 teaspoons avocado oil

2 tablespoons coconut aminos or 1/4 cup gluten-free soy sauce

1/4 cup powdered erythritol

- For The Tenderloin: Preheat the oven to 425° F (218°C).
- Mix sweetener and spices together.
- Brush tenderloin with oil on all sides and then rub with the spice mix.
- Place on a baking sheet, folding the skinny ends beneath for uniform thickness.
- Bake in a preheated oven until an internal temperature reaches up to a temperature of 145°F (62°C). It will take approximately 18 minutes.
- Once done, remove and let it cool before slicing.
- For The Sauce: Combine together all the sauce ingredients in a small-sized bowl and stir well.
- Serve this delicious sauce with tenderloin.

Lamb Shanks in the Instant Pot

Serves: 2 / Preparation time: 10 minutes / Cooking time: 55 minutes

- 2 tablespoons avocado oil
- 1 teaspoon fresh chilis, chopped (to garnish)
- 2 lamb shanks, trimmed
- 1/4 cup fresh cilantro, to garnish
- 1 teaspoon kosher salt
- 1/8th teaspoon xanthan gum
- 1/4 teaspoon ground black pepper
- 1 tablespoon granulated erythritol
- 1 tablespoon dried onion flakes
- 2/3 cup water
- 1 tablespoon ground coriander
- 1/3 cup coconut milk
- 1 tablespoon smoked paprika
- 1 tablespoon tomato paste
- 1 tablespoon ground cumin
- 1 teaspoon fresh garlic, minced
- 1 teaspoon garam masala
- 1 tablespoon fresh ginger, minced

- Mix dried onion flakes, kosher salt, 1/4 teaspoon ground black pepper, 1 teaspoon garam masala, ground coriander, ground cumin, and 1 tablespoon smoked paprika in a small-sized bowl.
- Rub lamb shanks with this spice mixture on all sides, reserving extra spice mix.
- Turn on the setting of your Instant Pot to Sauté setting.
- Preheat oil in the pot and cook lambs until brown on all sides, for 5 to 6 minutes.
- Next, add in reserved spices, a tablespoon of fresh minced ginger, a teaspoon of minced garlic, and 1 tablespoon tomato paste—Cook for 2 minutes before adding 2/3 cup water and 1/3 cup coconut milk.
- Stir well and secure the lid of your pot, making sure the vent is closed.
- Cook for 45 minutes on manual high pressure.
- Once the timer goes off, turn off your pot and let it cool for 15 minutes. Then release pressure via the quick-release method carefully.

- Remove lamb to a plate and set your machine back to sauté mode.
- Whisk in 1/8th teaspoon xanthan gum and 1 tablespoon granulated erythritol. Simmer until thickened, for about 5 minutes, stirring often.
- Transfer lamb shanks back to the pot and turn until coated with sauce on all sides.
- Serve over cauliflower rice/puree, with the gravy poured over.
- You can garnish with chili and fresh cilantro if desired.

Jamaican Jerk Pork Roast

Serves: 12 / Preparation time: 5 minutes / Cooking time: 45 minutes

1/4 cup Jamaican Jerk spice blend (no sugar)

1/2 cup beef stock or broth

4 lbs. pork shoulder

1 tablespoon olive oil

- Brush roast with oil on all sides and then rub with Jamaican Jerk spice blend.
- Turn on the sauté mode of your Instant Pot machine and cook meat until browned on all sides.
- Next, add in 1/2 cup beef stock or broth.
- Secure the lid as per instructions and cook for 45 minutes on manual high pressure.
- Once done, release pressure carefully and shred the roast.
- It's ready to serve!

Low Carb Beef and Broccoli

Serves: 2 / Preparation time: 10 minutes / Cooking time: 15 minutes

1 teaspoon fresh garlic, minced and divided

Salt, to taste

8 oz. flank steak, sliced

1 teaspoon fresh ginger, minced

2.5 cups large florets of broccoli

Sesame seeds, for garnish

1/2 teaspoon sesame oil

1 1/2 tablespoons avocado oil, divided

Green onion, for garnish

1/4 cup coconut aminos

Cauliflower rice, cooked

1/4 cup reduced-sodium beef broth

- Whisk together ½ teaspoon garlic, ½ teaspoon ginger, and a tablespoon of coconut aminos in a medium-sized bowl. Add in beef, toss well, and refrigerate for an hour, covered.
- Add a tablespoon of oil to the pan and preheat over medium-high flame. Cook broccoli for about 3 to 5 minutes until it begins to soften, stirring constantly.
- Add in remaining ginger and garlic and continue cooking for a minute.
- Turn off the heat and cook for about 4-5 minutes, until broccoli is tender, occasionally stirring, covered.
- Once done, remove broccoli to a plate and raise the temperature to medium-high.
- Add remaining half tablespoon of oil along with marinated beef and cook for a few minutes, until beef is golden brown on all sides. Then stir in broccoli.
- Whisk together 1/2 teaspoon sesame oil, 1/4 cup reduced-sodium beef broth, and remaining coconut aminos. Pour this mixture into a pan.
- Cook for two minutes , stirring frequently.
- Add salt to your preference.

- Serve delicious, warm keto beef over cauliflower rice with sesame seeds and green onion.

Poultry

Thai Chicken with Basil & Cauliflower Fried Rice

Serves: 4 / Preparation time: 10 minutes / Cooking time: 20 minutes

For the Cauliflower Fried Rice:

2 teaspoons fresh garlic, minced

2 tablespoons sugar-free fish sauce

1 teaspoon sesame oil

4 cups cauliflower, finely chopped (riced)

2 tablespoons avocado oil (or other lightly flavored)

1 tablespoon fresh ginger, minced

For the Thai Chicken with Basil:

2 tablespoons fresh chilis, minced

1/3 cup fresh basil leaves, chopped

2 tablespoons avocado) oil (or other lightly flavored

1 teaspoon granulated sugar substitute

3 cloves fresh garlic, chopped

2 tablespoons fish sauce

1 teaspoon fresh ginger, minced

2 cups raw chicken breast, chopped

Fried eggs to serve (optional)

- To Prepare Cauliflower Fried Rice: Preheat avocado oil and sesame oil in a cast-iron sauté pan over medium-high heat.
- Add in 2 teaspoons minced garlic and 1 tablespoon minced ginger. Cook for a minute and then add in stir-cook cauliflower for about 3 minutes.
- Stir in 2 tablespoons sugar-free fish sauce for about 3 minutes or until most of the liquid has evaporated.
- Once done, transfer the cauliflower to a serving platter.
- To Prepare Thai Chicken with Basil: In the same sauté pan, preheat avocado oil.
- Add in 3 chopped cloves of garlic, a teaspoon of minced ginger, and 2 tablespoons minced chilis. Cook until fragrant for a minute or two.
- Add in chicken and cook until cooked through and golden brown, stirring occasionally. It may take 5 to 6 minutes.

- Next, add a teaspoon of granulated sugar substitute, 2 tablespoons fish sauce, and 1/4 cup freshly chopped basil leaves. Stir and cook for 2 to 3 minutes.
- Once done, turn the heat off and serve over cauliflower.
- You can also serve with a fried egg.
- Enjoy this delicious keto Mediterranean meal!

Green Chicken Enchilada Cauliflower Casserole

Serves: 6 / Preparation time: 10 minutes / Cooking time: 35 minutes

1/2 teaspoon kosher salt

1 tablespoon fresh cilantro, chopped (optional)

20 oz. (about 4 cups) frozen cauliflower florets

1/4 cup sour cream

4 oz. cream cheese softened

1 cup sharp cheddar cheese, shredded

2 cups chicken, cooked and shredded

1/8 teaspoon ground black pepper

1/2 cup Salsa Verde

- Cook cauliflower in a microwave-safe dish until fork tender. It will take around 10 to 12 minutes.
- Add in cream cheese and continue cooking for another 30 seconds. Stir well.
- Next, add in 1/2 cup Salsa Verde, a cup of shredded cheddar cheese, a tablespoon of freshly chopped cilantro, 1/4 cup sour cream, 1/2 teaspoon kosher salt, 1/8 teaspoon ground black pepper, and 2 cups of cooked and shredded chicken. Stir well.
- Bake in a preheated oven at 375°F (190°C) for 20 minutes in an ovenproof casserole dish. Alternatively, microwave for 10 minutes on high.
- Serve and enjoy!

Chicken Nugget Meatballs

Serves: 16 / Preparation time: 5 minutes / Cooking time: 10 minutes

For The Meatball Mix:

1/8 teaspoon ground pepper

1/4 teaspoon paprika

1 lb. ground chicken or turkey

1/4 teaspoon fresh rosemary, minced

1/2 cup almond flour

1/8 teaspoon celery seeds

1 egg

1/2 teaspoon onion powder

1/2 teaspoon kosher salt

For The Coating:

3/4 teaspoon kosher salt

1/4 teaspoon paprika

1/2 cup almond flour

1/8 teaspoon garlic powder

2 tablespoons coconut flour

To Assemble And Fry:

2 tablespoons oil for frying

1 egg, beaten

For The Chipotle Mayonnaise:

1 teaspoon sriracha hot sauce

¼ cup mayonnaise

For The Honey Mustard:

1/4 cup honey

1/4 cup mustard

- To Prepare Meatball Mix: Add all the meatball ingredients to a large-sized bowl and mix well. Chill for about 10 minutes.
- Grease your hands lightly with oil and shape them into 16 meatballs.
- To Assembly And Fry: Add all the coating ingredients to a medium-sized bowl and combine well.
- Preheat oil in a nonstick pan.
- Start dipping meatballs, one by one, first into an egg and then into the coating mixture.
- Cook until golden brown on all sides, each side for 3 minutes.
- Serve with chipotle mayonnaise or honey mustard.

- To Prepare Chipotle Mayonnaise: Combine together sriracha hot sauce and mayonnaise.
- To Prepare Honey Mustard: Combine together honey and mustard.

Chicken Cacciatore Meatballs

Serves :4 / Preparation time: 15 minutes / Cooking time: 1 hour 5 minutes

For The Meatballs:

1 teaspoon kosher salt

1 tablespoon dried parsley flakes

1lb. ground chicken or turkey

1/2 teaspoon garlic powder

1 egg

1/4 teaspoon ground black pepper

1/3 cup almond flour

For The Sauce:

1/2 cup dry white wine (optional)

Grated parmesan to garnish (optional)

2 tablespoons olive oil

1 teaspoon dried parsley

1 cup cremini mushrooms, sliced

1 teaspoon dried oregano

1/2 cup onions, sliced

1 tablespoon capers, drained

1 1/2 cup red and yellow bell peppers, sliced

1 cup canned chopped tomatoes

2 cloves garlic, minced

1 cup chicken broth

- Add all the meatball ingredients to a large-sized bowl and mix well. Shape into 12 balls.
- Preheat oil in a sauté pan and cook meatballs, each side for 2 to 3 minutes, or until golden brown on all sides.
- Once done, remove meatballs from the pan.
- Add mushrooms to the same pan and cook each side for 2 to 3 minutes. Remove to a dish with cooked meatballs.
- Add in sliced peppers and onions and cook for about 4 minutes, until softened. Add a little oil, if desired.
- Add 2 minced cloves of garlic and cook until fragrant for a minute or two. Remove everything to a bowl with meatballs and mushrooms.
- Deglaze this pan with 1/2 cup dry white wine, scraping up browned bits from the bottom.

- Add a cup of broth and bring to a boil.
- Turn the heat down and add in herbs and tomatoes. Cook for about 2 minutes and then add in cooked veggies and meatballs with the sauce. Stir well.
- Adjust pepper and salt, if desired.
- Simmer everything at low for about half an hour.
- Serve warm over spaghetti squash or zucchini noodles.
- Finish with a sprinkle of grated parmesan and fresh parsley.

Chicken Salad with Greek Yogurt

Serves: 4 / Preparation time: 10 minutes / Cooking time: 15 minutes

1 tablespoon fresh lemon juice

2 teaspoons Italian seasoning

1 lb. chicken breast, cut into quarters

1/4 cup red onion, minced

2 1/2 cups sodium-reduced chicken stock

2 tablespoons pine nuts

2 cups water

1/2 cup sundried tomatoes, lightly packed in olive oil with herbs, minced

2 bay leaves

Black pepper, to taste

1/2 cup plain Greek non-fat yogurt

1/2 teaspoon salt

1/2 cup fresh basil, packed and roughly chopped

1 cup (about 12 hearts) artichoke Hearts, roughly chopped and divided (packed in water)

1 tablespoon garlic, minced

- Add chicken to a large pot and cover with water, broth, and bay leaves. Make sure to cover the chicken with about an inch of liquid.
- Turn on the flame over medium-high and cook until it just begins to simmer. Turn the heat down and cook the chicken for 12 to 15 minutes until the chicken comes to 160°F (73°C). Once done, remove to a bowl, straining a bit of liquid over the chicken top. Let the chicken rest for a few minutes.
- In the meantime, pulse ½ cup Artichoke hearts, a tablespoon of fresh lemon juice, 1/2 cup plain Greek non-fat yogurt, 1/2 teaspoon salt, pepper, a tablespoon of minced garlic, and ½ cup roughly chopped basil leaves in a food processor, until smooth, scraping down the sides if desired.
- Once the chicken is cool enough to handle, shred it with 2 forks. You should have about 2 3/4 cups of shredded chicken.
- Add chicken to a yogurt mixture along with 1/2 cup sundried tomatoes, 2 tablespoons pine nuts, 2 teaspoons Italian seasoning, and 1/4 cup minced red onion.
- Chop remaining artichokes finely and add them to a bowl.

- Stir well and adjust with pepper and salt, to taste.

Oven-Roasted Za'atar Chicken Breasts

Serves: 4 / Preparation time: 5 minutes / Cooking time: 25 minutes

2 tablespoons olive oil

Salt, to taste

4 boneless, skinless chicken breasts, pound into a thickness of an inch

Cooking spray

3 tablespoons za'atar seasoning, divided

1 clove garlic, minced

2 tablespoons lemon juice

- Add chicken to a large resealable plastic bag.
- Mix together 2 tablespoons lemon juice, one minced clove of garlic, 2 tablespoons olive oil, and 2 tablespoons za'atar seasoning in a small-sized bowl. Pour over chicken and toss until coated. Seal the bag and refrigerate for 2 hours at least.
- Preheat your oven to a temperature of 400°F (200°C).
- Take a baking sheet and line it with aluminum foil—grease with cooking spray.
- Place chicken on this baking sheet and sprinkle top with leftover za'atar seasoning.
- Roast for about 23 to 25 minutes, until chicken is no longer pink and cooked through.
- The internal temperature of the chicken should be at least 165 degrees F (74 degrees C)
- Sprinkle with a bit of salt and serve warm!

Chicken Pesto Stew with Zoodles

Serves: 4 / Preparation time: 10 minutes / Cooking time: 20 minutes

1 cup heavy whipping cream

Salt and ground black pepper, to taste

2 tablespoons butter

8 oz. (1¼ cups) tomatoes, diced, or cherry tomatoes cut in half

1½ lbs. boneless, skinless, boneless chicken thighs, cut into 1-inch pieces

1 lb. zucchini, spiralized

1½ teaspoons garlic powder

3 tablespoons green pesto

- Add butter to a frying pan and cook until melted.
- Once started bubbling, add in the chicken along with 1½ teaspoons of garlic powder. Sauté until lightly browned, for about 10 minutes.
- Turn the heat down and add in 3 tablespoons green pesto and 1 cup heavy whipping cream. Simmer until mixture is creamy, for a few minutes, stirring.
- Add in tomatoes and zucchini noodles. Toss well and continue simmering for another 2 to 3 minutes.
- Season with pepper and salt to taste.
- Serve right away!

Italian Chicken Parmesan with Cabbage Pasta

Serves: 4 / Preparation time: 15 minutes / Cooking time: 30 minutes

Italian Chicken Stew:

1 garlic clove, finely chopped

Salt and pepper

2 tablespoons butter for frying

1 cup (1 oz.) baby spinach

1½ lbs. boneless chicken thighs, sliced

1¼ cups (3½ oz.) Parmesan cheese, shredded

¼ cup (1 oz.) sun-dried tomatoes in oil, coarsely chopped

¾ cup heavy whipping cream

6 (3½ oz.) cherry tomatoes, cut into quarters

Cabbage Pasta:

11 oz. green cabbage, shredded

Salt or pepper

2 tablespoons butter for frying

- Preheat butter in a pan and fry chicken until thoroughly cooked for a couple of minutes.
- Season the chicken with pepper and salt to taste.
- Add in finely chopped garlic, tomatoes, and ¾ cup heavy whipping cream. Simmer for about 5 minutes, over medium heat.
- Add in 1¼ cups shredded parmesan and continue simmering for another 10 minutes. Adjust salt and pepper at this step, if desired.
- To Prepare Cabbage Pasta: In the meantime, melt butter in a large frying pan.
- Add in shredded cabbage and cook until tender. Season the cabbage with pepper and salt to your preference.
- Just before serving, stir spinach into a pan with cream chicken.
- Spread cabbage onto a plate and top with delicious and warm creamy chicken sauce.

Pesto Chicken Casserole With Feta Cheese And Olives

Serves: 4 / Preparation time: 15 minutes / Cooking time: 30 minutes

1⁄3 cup (2¾ oz.) red pesto or green pesto

1 garlic clove, finely chopped

1½ lbs. boneless chicken thighs, cut into bite-sized pieces

5 oz. (1 cup) feta cheese, diced

Salt and pepper

3 oz. (2⁄3 cup) olives pitted

2 tablespoons butter or coconut oil

1¼ cups heavy whipping cream

5 oz. (2½ cups) leafy greens, for serving

- Preheat your oven to a temperature of 400°F (200°C).
- Season the chicken pieces with pepper and salt.
- Add oil or butter to a large skillet, add in seasoned chicken and fry until golden brown on all sides. Do this in batches, if desired.
- In a medium-sized bowl, mix together heavy cream and pesto.
- Place chicken pieces in a baking dish along with diced feta cheese, chopped garlic, and pitted olives.
- Top with the cream-pesto mixture.
- Bake until edges become light brown and the top is bubbly, for about 20 to 30 minutes.
- Remove and serve immediately.

Creamy Tuscan Garlic Chicken

Serves: 6 / Preparation time: 10 minutes / Cooking time: 15 minutes

1 teaspoon garlic powder

1/2 cup sun-dried tomatoes

1½ lbs. chicken breasts, boneless and skinless (sliced)

1 cup spinach, chopped

2 tablespoons olive oil

1/2 cup parmesan cheese

1 cup heavy cream

1 teaspoon Italian seasoning

1/2 cup chicken broth

- Preheat olive oil in a large skillet and cook chicken until brown on all sides and no longer pink, each side for 3 to 5 minutes.
- Once done, remove and keep it aside.
- Whisk in 1 teaspoon Italian seasoning, 1/2 cup chicken broth, 1/2 cup parmesan cheese, 1 teaspoon garlic powder, and 1 cup heavy cream until it begins to thicken.
- Add in sundried tomatoes and spinach and continue simmering until spinach has wilted.
- Transfer chicken back to the pan and serve over pasta.

BBQ Chicken Low Carb Healthy Quesadillas

Serves: 2 / Preparation time: 20 minutes / Cooking time: 15 minutes

2 cups liquid egg whites

2-4 tablespoons cilantro, chopped

1 cup chicken breast, shredded

2/3 cup cheddar cheese, grated

Avocado oil spray

1/4 cup BBQ sauce of choice + more for drizzling (low carb if desired)

- Cook chicken breast in a pot of salted water for about 10 to 15 minutes, until no longer pink from inside. Once done, remove from pot and set it aside.
- Preheat the broiler to high and adjust the rack of your oven to the 2nd from the top.
- Take a baking sheet and spray with avocado oil spray.
- Take a small pan and spray with avocado oil. Turn on the flame. Once hot, reduce the flame and pour in 1/2 cup of the egg whites slowly and gradually.
- Cook for about 5 minutes, until egg top, is set. Once done, slide the egg into a prepared baking sheet.
- Cook remaining egg whites similarly until you have 4 "tortillas."
- Once done, place all egg tortillas onto the prepared baking sheet and spray top with avocado oil.
- Shred chicken by using forks and transfer to a bowl.
- Mix in 1/4 cup BBQ sauce until chicken is coated.
- Divide chicken between two of the egg tortillas and spread out evenly until the entire tortilla has covered.
- Top with cheese and cilantro, and again spray with avocado oil.
- Cover with additional tortillas in a way that the uncooked side of the egg white remains down.
- Spray tops with avocado oil.

- Place under broiler and broil for about 15 minutes, until egg whites begin to bubble.
- Enjoy delicious keto-Mediterranean Quesadillas!

Everything Bagel Chicken Recipe

Serves: 4 / Preparation time: 10 minutes / Cooking time: 25 minutes

8 teaspoons everything but the bagel sesame seasoning blend

1 tablespoon olive oil

1 lb. (4 small breasts) boneless skinless chicken breast

4 tablespoons cream cheese

- Preheat the oven to 350°F 1(76°C).
- Start slicing chicken breasts almost all the way (open width-wise). Two sides should still be joined together. Season the chicken with a pinch of salt.
- Sprinkle bagel seasoning over all sides of breasts.
- Drop a tablespoon of cheese at the end of each piece of chicken breast and roll up, securing with toothpicks.
- Preheat oil in an oven-safe frying pan and sear chicken for about 3 to 4 minutes, until browned on all sides.
- Place the pan inside a preheated oven and cook further for about 15 to 20 minutes until an instant-read thermometer reaches a temperature of 165°F (73°C).
- Serve right away!

Chicken Parmesan Casserole

Serves: 8 / Preparation time: 10 minutes / Cooking time: 40 minutes

For The Chicken:

1/2 teaspoon kosher salt

1 teaspoon dried parsley

1/2 teaspoon garlic powder

1/4 cup parmesan cheese, grated

1/2 teaspoon dried basil

1/8 teaspoon ground black pepper

3 tablespoons olive oil for frying

1.5 lbs. chicken breast, boneless, cut into 2-inch pieces

1 egg

1/2 cup almond flour

For The Casserole:

1/8 teaspoon ground black pepper

Fresh basil, chopped (optional for garnish)

4 cups cooked spaghetti squash, well-drained

6 oz. fresh mozzarella, cut or tear into pieces

1 tablespoon olive oil

1.5 cups easy keto marinara sauce

1/2 teaspoon kosher salt

1/2 tablespoon dried parsley

- Beat egg in a small-sized bowl.
- Combine together the first six ingredients of chicken in a medium-sized bowl.
- Now start dipping the chicken pieces, one by one, first into a beaten egg and then into a coating mixture.
- Preheat oil in a nonstick pan and cook chicken pieces until golden brown on all sides. Once done, remove to a plate lined with a clean paper towel.
- For The Casserole:
- Combine together spaghetti, parsley, pepper, salt, and oil in a medium-sized bowl.
- Spread the squash out in an oven-safe dish (8 x 12).
- Spread top of squash with cooked chicken pieces.

- Spoon over marinara sauce followed by mozzarella pieces on top.
- Bake for about half an hour at 375 degrees F (190.556°C), or until cheese is melted.
- Finish with a garnish of freshly chopped basil and serve immediately.

Pistachio Crusted Chicken With Coriander Yogurt Sauce

Serves: 2 / Preparation time: 15 minutes / Cooking time: 15 minutes

For The Chicken:

Salt

8 oz. (2 small breasts) chicken

1/2 cup roasted pistachios

1 large egg white

For The Cauliflower Rice:

cilantro, for garnish

Fresh lime juice, to taste

4 cups cauliflower, cut into bite-sized pieces

Salt/pepper, to taste

For The Sauce:

Juice of half a lime

Pinch of salt

1/2 cup plain, non-fat Greek yogurt

1/8 teaspoon cayenne pepper

1/2 teaspoon ground coriander

- Preheat oven to 425 °F (218°C).
- Place a small cooling rack over a large baking sheet.
- Grind pistachios in a food processor with a pinch of salt until pistachios are broken down but still chunky.
- Transfer pistachios to a shallow plate having edges.
- Beat egg into a separate bowl.
- Pat dry the chicken with clean paper towels and dip into a beaten egg, shaking off excess, if any.
- Then coat chicken with pistachios, rolling around gently until chicken is covered on all sides, lightly pressing with your hands.
- Place the coated chicken onto the positioned rack and cook for about 12 to 15 minutes until the outside of the chicken is crunchy and golden brown.
- In the meantime, process cauliflower in a food processor until it resembles rice.

- Add cauliflower rice to a bowl and microwave for 3 to 4 minutes, until softened.
- Toss with roughly chopped cilantro lime juice.
- Season with pepper and salt to taste.
- To make a sauce, whisk together all the sauce ingredients and serve over cauliflower rice & chicken.
- Finish with a garnishing of cilantro and enjoy!

Chicken Cordon Bleu Meatballs

Serves: 16 / Preparation time: 10 minutes / Cooking time: 10 minutes

For The Meatballs:

1/4 teaspoon black pepper

Oil, for frying

1 lb. ground chicken or turkey

16 (1/2 inch) squares Swiss cheese or other

1 egg

4 slices deli ham, finely chopped

1/3 cup almond flour

1 tablespoon dried parsley

1/4 cup grated Parmesan cheese

1/2 teaspoon garlic powder

1/2 teaspoon kosher salt

1/2 teaspoon paprika

For The Coating:

1/3 cup coconut flour

1/4 teaspoon paprika

1 egg, beaten

1/2 teaspoon kosher salt

For The Sauce:

1/4 cup sour cream

1 teaspoon Dijon mustard

1/4 cup mayonnaise

2 tablespoons dill pickle, chopped (or dill pickle relish)

- To Prepare Meatballs: Add all the meatball ingredients to a large-sized bowl and mix well. Shape into 16 balls.
- Press a square of cheese into the center of each ball, reforming meat around the cheese evenly using your hands.
- Mix together 1/3 cup coconut flour, 1/2 teaspoon kosher salt, and 1/4 teaspoon paprika in a small-sized bowl.
- Crack an egg into another bowl and beat well.
- Add oil to a nonstick pan to a depth of about half an inch. Turn on the flame and allow it to preheat. Once hot, dip meatballs first into an egg mixture and then coat with coconut flour mix on all sides.

- Fry each side for about 3 minutes, until golden brown.
- Once done, remove from pan and remove to a plate lined with a paper towel.
- To Prepare the Sauce: Mix all the sauce ingredients in a bowl. Simple as that!

Thai Chicken Salad

Serves: 4 / Preparation time: 15 minutes / Cooking time: 15 minutes

- 1 shallot, thinly sliced
- Fresh chili, to serve
- 2 tablespoons sesame seeds
- 12 lettuce leaves baby romaine or butter
- 2 tablespoons fish sauce
- ½ cup cilantro leaves
- 1 tablespoon water
- ½ cup mint leaves
- 1 lb. ground chicken thigh
- 2 scallions, thinly sliced
- 2 tablespoons sesame oil
- 1 lime, juiced
- 1 tablespoon lemongrass, ground into a paste
- 1 teaspoon ground galangal
- 2 cloves garlic, crushed

- Add sesame seeds to a large saucepan/wok and toast until lightly browned.
- Transfer seeds to a spice grinder or mortar and pestle and crush until you have a mixture like fine breadcrumbs. Keep it aside.
- Add fish sauce to the same wok along with water and chicken. Sauté the chicken until cooked, but not browned, breaking up.
- Add in lemongrass, sesame oil, and garlic and continue cooking for another minute. Turn the heat off.
- Stir in lime juice, galangal, and shallot, and let everything cool for a few minutes before adding ground sesame seeds, cilantro, mint, and scallions. Combine well.
- Spoon this mixture into the lettuce leaves evenly, followed by fresh chili on top.
- Serve right away!

Chicken Tamale Casserole

Serves: 6 / Preparation time: 15 minutes / Cooking time: 40 minutes

Cornbread Base Ingredients:

1 jalapeno, finely chopped

4 drops corn flavoring

1 cup almond flour

2 large eggs

1 teaspoon baking powder

2 tablespoons heavy cream

1 teaspoon erythritol

¼ cup salted butter, melted

½ teaspoon salt

Mexican Chicken Topping Ingredients:

2 teaspoons taco seasoning

Sour cream, to serve

1 cup keto enchilada sauce

1 scallion, sliced

10 oz. chicken, cooked and shredded

1 cup Monterey jack cheese, shredded

- Preheat the oven to 375°F (190°C).
- Combine 1 teaspoon baking powder, 1 cup almond flour, finely chopped jalapeno, ½ teaspoon salt, and 1 teaspoon erythritol in a medium-sized bowl.
- Add in 2 large eggs, 2 tablespoons heavy cream, ¼ cup melted butter, and 4 drops of corn flavoring.
- Take out a casserole dish and grease it with olive oil spray.
- Pour cornbread mix into a dish and smooth the top evenly.
- Bake until golden brown for 14 minutes.
- Poke holes in the cornbread using a chopstick, then pour over half of the enchilada sauce. Keep it aside.
- Add chicken to a bowl and toss with remaining enchilada sauce and taco seasoning.
- Spoon chicken-taco mixture over cornbread followed by cheese on top.
- Bake until cheese is browned, for 15 to 20 minutes.

- Garnish with sliced scallion and enjoy with a dollop of sour cream, if needed.

Chicken & Cauliflower Soup

Serves: 8 / Preparation time: 10 minutes / Cooking time: 40 minutes

2 cloves garlic, crushed

2 tablespoons mint, finely chopped (to serve)

12 oz. chicken thighs

Salt, to taste

1 tablespoon olive oil

5 oz. feta cheese, crumbled

1 lemon zest and juice

1/2 teaspoon pepper

1/2 teaspoon salt

1 cup chicken stock

2 oz. butter

21 oz. heavy cream

1 tablespoon oregano dried

1.6 lbs. cauliflower, cut into florets

1 small onion, diced

- Preheat the oven to 390 °F (198°C).
- Place chicken in a roasting tray and drizzle top with oil. Sprinkle with salt and lemon zest, and salt in a preheated oven until chicken is cooked through and browned for 15 to 20 minutes.
- Once done, shred the chicken into small pieces and keep them aside.
- Add butter to a large saucepan over high heat and onion, oregano, and garlic. Cook until onion is translucent, stirring occasionally.
- Place a large saucepan over high heat.
- Stir in cauliflower for 2 minutes, and then add in chicken stock and heavy cream. Turn the heat down and simmer until cauliflower is tender. It may take 15 to 20 minutes.
- Using a stick blender, blend the cauliflower carefully until no lumps remain.
- Add in lemon juice, pepper, and shredded chicken and stir well.
- Stir in crumbled cheese and adjust the salt, if needed.
- Ladle delicious chicken and cauliflower soup into serving bowls and garnish with mint just before serving.

Peanut Chicken Tenders

Serves:4 / Preparation time: 10 minutes / Cooking time: 20 minutes

For The Chicken Tenders:

1/4 teaspoon cayenne pepper

1 teaspoon grated lime zest

1 lb. raw chicken tenders

1 tablespoon sriracha hot sauce

1/2 cup dry roasted peanuts

1 teaspoon ginger, minced

1 teaspoon kosher salt

1/4 cup mayonnaise

For The Dipping Sauce:

1 tablespoon sesame oil

2 tablespoons avocado oil

2 tablespoons lime juice

1 tablespoon granulated erythritol sweetener

1 tablespoon fish sauce

- Preheat the oven to 375°F (190°C).
- Add 1/2 cup dry roasted peanuts to a food processor along with 1/4 teaspoon cayenne pepper and 1 teaspoon kosher salt to a food processor. Pulse until it resembles coarse crumbs.
- In a bowl, mix together hot sriracha sauce, 1/4 cup mayonnaise, 1 teaspoon grated lime zest, and a teaspoon of minced ginger.
- Stir in chicken tenders until coated with the mayonnaise mixture on all sides.
- Transfer peanut coating to a large plate and start rolling chicken tenders one by one in the peanut mixture. Then place in an oil sheet pan.
- Bake in a preheated oven until tenders have golden brown and cooked through. It may take 20 minutes.
- To prepare the dipping sauce, whisk together all the sauce ingredients in a small-sized bowl and serve with warm chicken tenders.

Caesar Baked Chicken

Serves: 4 / Preparation time: 5 minutes / Cooking time: 1 hour 5 minutes

1 teaspoon lemon juice

1/4 teaspoon onion powder

4 chicken thighs (or you can use other chicken pieces)

1/4 teaspoon garlic powder

1/4 cup Caesar salad dressing

1 teaspoon kosher salt

- Mix together lemon juice, Caesar salad dressing, garlic powder, onion powder, and kosher salt in a medium-sized bowl.
- Add in chicken and rub the marinade into thighs and under the skin, too, if possible.
- Refrigerate for at least 2 hours, covered.
- After taking it out of the refrigerator, preheat your oven to a temperature of 400°F (204°C).
- Place chicken onto a sheet pan lined with foil or parchment.
- Bake until chicken is cooked through and crispy for an hour. Cook until an internal temperature reaches 165 degrees F (73°C) for about 25 minutes
- for boneless chicken.
-

Chicken & Chorizo Sheet Pan Dinner

Serves: 4 / Preparation time: 10 minutes / Cooking time: 45 minutes

1 tablespoon avocado or olive oil

1/2 teaspoon dried thyme leaves

4 bone-in chicken thighs

1 teaspoon garlic powder

4 links of raw Mexican chorizo

1/4 teaspoon ground black pepper

4 cups zucchini, sliced

1 teaspoon kosher salt

1 cup cherry tomatoes

- Preheat the oven to 400°F (204°C)
- Season the chicken with a generous amount of pepper and salt on all sides.
- Now evenly distribute the seasoned chicken across a large sheet pan along with sliced zucchini, 4 links of raw Mexican chorizo, and tomatoes.
- Drizzle top with oil and sprinkle with 1/4 of teaspoon pepper, a teaspoon of salt, garlic powder, and dried thyme leaves.
- Bake in a preheated oven until the internal temperature of the chicken reaches 160°F (71°C). It will take 35 to 40 minutes.
- Slice the chorizo into thick coins of ½ inch and serve with chicken and vegetables.

Easy Keto Chicken Shawarma

Serves: 6 / Preparation time: 25 minutes / Cooking time: 10 minutes

For The Chicken Shawarma:

1 tablespoon smoked paprika

3 tablespoons olive oil

2 lbs. boneless chicken breast or thighs

2 tablespoons lemon juice

1 teaspoon ground coriander

1/4 teaspoon ground black pepper

1 teaspoon ground cumin

1.5 teaspoons kosher salt

1 teaspoon ground cardamom

1/2 teaspoon onion powder

1 teaspoon ground turmeric

1/2 teaspoon garlic powder

1/2 teaspoon ground cayenne pepper

For The Tahini Sauce:

3 tablespoons water

1/2 teaspoon kosher salt

2 tablespoons tahini paste

1 clove garlic, minced

2 tablespoons olive oil

1 tablespoon lemon juice

- For The Chicken Shawarma: Add all the marinade ingredients to a large-sized bowl and mix well.
- Add in chicken, turn until coated on all sides and marinate for 2 hours at least or overnight.
- Preheat your grill to a temperature of 500 °F (260°C).
- Cook chicken over direct heat each side for 4 minutes or until an internal temperature reaches up to 160°F (71°C).
- Once done, remove from grill and leave for 10 minutes.
- Once cooled enough to handle, slice and serve with tahini sauce.
- For The Tahini Sauce: Mix together all the sauce ingredients in a bowl. It's ready!

Belizean Stewed Chicken In The Instant Pot

Serves: 8 / Preparation time: 10 minutes / Cooking time: 25 minutes

2 cups chicken stock

4 whole chicken legs (drumsticks and thighs, separated into 8 pieces)

1 tablespoon granulated sugar substitute

1 tablespoon coconut oil

1/2 teaspoon ground black pepper

2 tablespoons achiote seasoning/paste

1 cup yellow onions, sliced

1 teaspoon dried oregano

2 tablespoons white vinegar

1 teaspoon ground cumin

3 tablespoons Worcestershire sauce

3 cloves garlic, sliced

- Mix together 3 tablespoons Worcestershire sauce, 1 tablespoon sugar substitute, 2 tablespoons achiote paste, 1 teaspoon dried oregano, 1 teaspoon ground cumin, 2 tablespoons white vinegar, and 1/2 teaspoon black pepper in a medium-sized bowl.
- Add in chicken pieces and rub the mixture into the skin.
- Marinate overnight or for an hour at least.
- Place insert in your Instant Pot machine and turn on its Sauté mode.
- Preheat coconut oil and cook chicken until browned, each side for 2 minutes. Do this in batches and reserve the marinade.
- Remove chicken to a plate and add garlic and onions to Instant Pot. Continue sautéing until softened for a few minutes. Transfer chicken back to the pot.
- Add 2 cups chicken stock to a bowl and stir it with reserved marinade. Pour into the pot.
- Seal your machine as per the manufacturer's directions and cook for 20 minutes on Manual-High Pressure.
- Once the cycle has been completed, allow releasing the steam naturally. It will take some time.
- Carefully put off the lid and adjust the salt, if desired.

- Remove chicken to a serving platter and garnish with cilantro.

Chicken Souvlaki With Yogurt Sauce

Serves: 4 / Preparation time: 10 minutes / Cooking time: 5-10 minutes

For The Chicken:

1 tablespoon fresh oregano, chopped

1/2 teaspoon dried thyme

1 lb. chicken breast, cut into strips

1/4 teaspoon ground black pepper

3 tablespoons olive oil

2 teaspoons kosher salt

3 tablespoons lemon juice

4 cloves garlic, minced

1 tablespoon red wine vinegar

For The Yogurt Sauce:

1 teaspoon garlic, minced

1/2 teaspoon granulated sugar substitute

3/4 cup Greek yogurt

1/2 teaspoon kosher salt

1 teaspoon lemon juice

1 teaspoon fresh oregano, chopped

- To Make The Chicken: Add all the chicken ingredients to a non-reactive dish except for chicken and mix well.
- Add in chicken strips and mix well until coated with the marinade.
- Marinate for 2 hours in the refrigerator, covered.
- Thread chicken onto skewers after removing from marinade.
- Grill chicken onto a preheated grill, each side for 2 minutes. Time may vary, depending upon the thickness of chicken pieces.
- Serve warm with yogurt sauce.
- To Make The Yogurt Sauce: Mix together all the sauce ingredients in a bowl. It's ready to serve!

Instant Pot Turmeric Chicken and Vegetables

Serves: 2 / Preparation time: 5 minutes / Cooking time: 5 minutes

1/4 teaspoon ground cinnamon

Cilantro, for garnish

2 tablespoons coconut oil, melted and divided

1/2 red bell pepper, cut into very small pieces

8 oz. chicken breast, cubed

1 cup broccoli, cut into very small pieces

1/2 cup light coconut milk

1 cup small Brussels sprouts, trimmed

2 teaspoons tomato paste

Pinch of pepper

1 teaspoon fresh ginger, minced

1/4 teaspoon salt

3/4 teaspoon ground turmeric

- Add 1 1/2 tablespoons of coconut oil to your Instant Pot and turn on its Sauté mode.
- Cook chicken for 4 to 5 minutes, until no longer pink from inside and golden from outside.
- In the meantime, combine together 1/2 cup light coconut milk, 1 teaspoon of fresh minced ginger, 2 teaspoons of tomato paste,1/4 teaspoon ground cinnamon, 3/4 teaspoon of ground turmeric, a pinch of pepper, 1/4 teaspoon of salt, and remaining oil.
- Once the chicken is cooked, add this mixture into your Instant Pot.
- Stir in Brussels sprouts until coated with sauce. Secure the lid of your pot, setting it to a sealing position.
- Cook for a minute on manual-high pressure.
- Once the timer goes off, do release the steam via the Quick release method.
- Once released, stir in peppers and broccoli.
- Put on the lid and let everything sit until veggies are steamed, for 20 to 25 minutes.
- Finish with a garnish of cilantro and enjoy!

Chicken Piccata Meatballs

Serves: 5 / Preparation time: 15minutes / Cooking time: 15 minutes

For The Meatballs:

1/4 teaspoon ground black pepper

2 tablespoons olive oil for frying

1 lb. ground chicken or turkey

1 teaspoon fresh parsley, chopped

1/3 cup almond flour

1/2 teaspoon lemon zest

1/2 teaspoon lemon zest

1 egg

1/4 teaspoon garlic powder

1/2 teaspoon kosher salt

For The Sauce:

2 tablespoons capers, drained and roughly chopped

1/4 cup butter

1/2 cup dry white wine

1/4 teaspoon lemon zest

2 tablespoons lemon juice

- To Make The Meatballs: Combine together all the meatball ingredients except for oil in a large-sized bowl and shape into 15 meatballs.
- Fry in hot oil until cooked through and golden brown. Once done, remove to a plate and keep warm.
- To Make The Sauce: Add white wine to the same pan and bring to a boil, scraping all the bits off of the bottom.
- Add in 2 tablespoons of capers and 2 tablespoons lemon juice and cook for 2 to 3 minutes, until reduced by half.
- Turn off the heat and stir in 1/4 cup butter and 1/4 teaspoon lemon zest.
- Adjust the taste with pepper and salt to taste.
- Serve meatballs with hot & delicious sauce!
- Wow, what a fantastic low-carb keto Mediterranean meal!

Asparagus Stuffed Chicken Breast

Serves: 4 / Preparation time: 10 minutes / Cooking time: 20 minutes

Sea salt

1 tablespoon olive oil

1 lb. (about 4 small breasts) chicken breast

8 Stalks of asparagus, trimmed to fit in the chicken

Italian seasoning

3 oz. Provolone cheese (4 thick slices)

Garlic powder

4 teaspoons Honey mustard

- First, preheat your oven to a temperature of 425°F (218 °C).
- Slice chicken breast pieces in half all the way, but keep them still intact.
- Sprinkle the inside of each breast piece with garlic powder, Italian seasoning, and a pinch of salt without measuring. Sprinkle the outside with just Italian seasoning.
- Spread a teaspoon of honey mustard all over the chicken breast pieces and top each with a slice of provolone, followed by 2asparagus spears. Fold over the chicken and secure it using toothpicks.
- Preheat oil in an oven-safe pan and cook chicken, each side, for 2 to 3 minutes, until golden brown.
- Cover this pan with tinfoil and bake for 15 minutes, or until an internal temperature reaches up to 165°F (73°C).
- Amazing!

Crock-Pot Slow Cooker Crack Chicken

Serves: 10 / Preparation time: 5 minutes / Cooking time: 3 hours

1 teaspoon onion powder

1/3 cup green onions, chopped

2 lbs. chicken breast

1/2 cup bacon bits, cooked

2 tablespoons dried parsley

1 cup cheddar cheese, shredded

1 tablespoon dried dill

16 oz. cream cheese, cut into pieces

1 tablespoon dried chives

1/2 teaspoon black pepper

1 teaspoon garlic powder

- Place chicken in a single layer in the slow cooker.
- Sprinkle with all spices and herbs, followed by pieces of cream cheese over the top.
- Cook for 6 to 8 hours on low of 3 to 4 hours on high.
- Once done, shred it and stir well.
- Stir in green onions, bacon bits, and shredded cheddar cheese.
- Crockpot slow cooker crack chicken is ready to serve!

Chicken Laksa Recipe

Serves: 2 / Preparation time: 15 minutes / Cooking time: 15 minutes

1 tablespoon fish sauce

Fresh mint leaves

8 oz. chicken thigh, thinly sliced

1 red chili, sliced

1 tablespoon coconut oil

1/2 cup bean sprouts

4 tablespoons low carb laksa paste

1 packet shirataki noodles

2 cups chicken stock

Erythritol, to taste

1 cup coconut cream

Salt, to taste

1 tablespoon lime juice

- Preheat coconut oil in a nonstick pan and cook chicken until browned on all sides. Once done, remove and set it aside.
- Add 4 tablespoons of low-carb laksa paste and sauté for about 3 to 5 minutes.
- Add in 2 cups of chicken stock and bring everything to a simmer.
- Transfer chicken back to the pan and add in 1 cup coconut cream, 1 tablespoon fish sauce, and 1 tablespoon lime juice. Stir well and simmer until chicken is cooked through.
- Adjust sweetener and salt to your preferences.
- Cook noodles as per directions mentioned in the package and divide among two bowls.
- Spoon over prepared laksa soup.
- Top each bowl with sliced chili, bean sprouts, and fresh mint leaves.
- Serve immediately!

Chicken & Cheese Casserole Bake

Serves: 6 / Preparation time: 15 minutes / Cooking time: 30 minutes

½ teaspoon white pepper ground

Fresh oregano, finely chopped (to serve)

2 tablespoons salted butter

1 cup cheddar cheese, shredded

1 onion, sliced

1 rotisserie chicken, shredded (600g of meat)

2 teaspoons garlic powder

3 cups baby spinach

2 teaspoons dried oregano

½ cup heavy cream

1 teaspoon smoked paprika

8 oz. cream cheese

1 teaspoon mustard powder

3 cups mushrooms, sliced

1 teaspoon salt

- Preheat the oven to 390 °F (198 °C).
- Sauté butter and onion for 3 minutes in a large saucepan.
- Add in salt, pepper, spices, and herbs and continue sautéing for another 2 minutes.
- Add in mushrooms and cook until softened.
- Next, add in ½ cup heavy cream and 8 oz. cream cheese and cook until cheese has melted.
- Bring everything to simmer, then stir in spinach. Once wilted, add in shredded chicken.
- Pour into a casserole dish, smooth out and top with a cup of shredded cheddar cheese.
- Bake in a preheated oven until cheese is golden brown, for 20 to 25 minutes.
- Remove to serving bowls and finish with a garnish of chopped oregano!

Chicken Drumsticks Indonesian Style

Serves: 4 / Preparation time: 5 minutes / Cooking time: 45 minutes

1/2 teaspoon pepper

2 tablespoons sesame oil

8 chicken drumsticks

1/2 teaspoon ginger ground

2 teaspoons turmeric ground

1/2 teaspoon cumin ground

1 teaspoon garlic powder

1/2 teaspoon coriander ground

1 teaspoon onion flakes

1/2 teaspoon chili powder

1 teaspoon salt

- Add all the ingredients to a bowl except for sesame oil and chicken drumsticks. Mix well.
- Rub chicken drumsticks with this seasoning mix and marinate for at least 2 hours or overnight.
- Preheat the oven to 390°F (198°C).
- Arrange chicken drumsticks on a parchment-lined baking tray and drizzle top with sesame oil.
- Bake in a preheated oven until drumsticks are cooked through, for 35 to 45 minutes.
- Enjoy with mayonnaise.

Spinach Stuffed Chicken Breast Recipe

Serves: 4 / Preparation time: 10 minutes / Cooking time: 20 minutes

Black pepper

4 large chicken breasts

Sea salt

6 oz. spinach, chopped

1 medium Roma tomato, sliced thinly into 8 slices

2 cloves garlic, minced

2 oz. cream cheese

4 oz. mozzarella cheese, shredded and divided

- Preheat the oven to 450°F (232°C).
- Take a baking sheet and line it with foil or parchment paper.
- Add water to a large bowl along with salt and place chicken inside. Brine the chicken breast pieces for 10 minutes.
- In the meantime, add spinach to a bowl and microwave for a few minutes. Once cooled enough, squeeze over the sink to squeeze out the liquid as much as possible. Transfer back to the bowl.
- Stir in 2 oz. of shredded mozzarella and 2 minced cloves of garlic. Microwave again; cheese is easy to stir.
- Pat the chicken dry after removing from water and place onto the prepared baking sheet, cutting a horizontal slit in each breast piece to create a pocket.
- Stuff each chicken pocket with spinach mixture and sprinkle with a little pepper and salt.
- Top each piece with 2 slices of tomato followed by 1/3 oz and shredded mozzarella cheese.
- Bake in a preheated oven until chicken is cooked through, for 16 to 20 minutes.

Baked Lemon Pepper Wings Recipe

Serves: 6 / Preparation time: 5 minutes / Cooking time: 45 minutes

2 teaspoons baking powder

3 lbs. chicken wings

1/4 cup lemon pepper seasoning

3 tablespoons olive oil

- Preheat the oven to 400°F (204°C).
- Fit two oven-safe racks into two rimmed baking sheets.
- Add chicken wings to a bowl and toss with oil until coated on all sides.
- Season all sides with 1/4 cup lemon pepper seasoning and toss with baking powder (optional).
- Arrange wings on the prepared racks, each with some gap.
- Bake until an internal temperature reaches up to 165 degrees F (73°C). It will take 40 to 45 minutes.
- Serve delicious lemon pepper chicken wings immediately!

Air Fryer Fried Chicken

Serves: 6 / Preparation time: 10 minutes / Cooking time: 20 minutes

2 large eggs

1/4 teaspoon dried thyme

2 1/2 lbs. chicken drumsticks

1/2 teaspoon garlic powder

1/4 cup wholesome yum coconut flour

1 teaspoon smoked paprika

1/2 teaspoon sea salt

1 cup pork rinds

1/4 teaspoon black pepper

- Mix together 1/2 teaspoon sea salt, 1/4 cup coconut flour, and 1/4 teaspoon black pepper in a shallow bowl. Keep it aside.
- Take another bowl and crack eggs into it. Beat well and set it aside too.
- In a third bowl, combine 1 teaspoon smoked paprika, 1 cup pork rinds, 1/4 teaspoon dried thyme, and 1/2 teaspoon garlic powder.
- Now, first, dredge chicken pieces into a mixture of coconut flour, then dip into beaten eggs, and finally into the pork rind mixture, shaking off the excess in every turn.
- Preheat your air fryer to a temperature of 400° F (204°C) for 5 minutes.
- Arrange breaded chicken pieces onto a greased metal basket in a single layer, each with some distance.
- Place the basket inside your air fryer and cook until the internal temperature reaches 165 degrees F (73.889°C). It will take approximately 20 minutes.
- Once done, serve as is!

Best Garlic Chicken Wings

Serves: 4 / Preparation time: 15 minutes / Cooking time: 15 minutes

1/2 teaspoon salt

Lemon wedges, to serve

10 chicken wings

3 oz. tallow

1 teaspoon garlic powder

1/2 teaspoon Pepper

- First, you have to separate the wings, keeping the middle section and drumettes. After discarding the tip, you'll have 20 pieces.
- Marinate wings with pepper, salt, and garlic powder. Leave for 15 minutes.
- To a large nonstick pan, add tallow and preheat over medium-high heat.
- Once melted, add in wings and fry for 5 minutes.
- Flip over, cover with a lid and continue frying for another 5 minutes.
- Put off the lid and cook for 5 minutes more.
- Cut through one piece and ensure the internal temperature is above 160°F (71°C), using a meat thermometer to check their doneness.
- If done, serve with lemon wedges.

Roasted Chicken And Vegetables In The Oven

Serves: 4 / Preparation time: 10 minutes / Cooking time: 25 minutes

For Chicken:

1 teaspoon paprika

1/4 teaspoon black pepper

2 lbs. boneless skinless chicken thighs

3/4 teaspoon sea salt

2 tablespoons olive oil

1/2 teaspoon garlic powder

1 teaspoon Italian seasoning

For Vegetables:

1/4 cup olive oil, divided

1/4 teaspoon black pepper

1 large bell pepper, cut into thin strips

3/4 teaspoon sea salt

4 oz. broccoli, cut into florets

1/2 teaspoon garlic powder

4 oz. cauliflower, cut into florets

1/2 teaspoon paprika

8 oz. zucchini, sliced into 1/4 inch thickness

1 teaspoon Italian seasoning

1/4 red onion, cut into pieces of 1-inch, layers separated

- First, preheat your oven to a temperature of 425°F (218°C).
- Line a baking sheet (extra-large) with foil or parchment paper.
- Arrange chicken thighs onto a baking sheet in a single layer. Brush both sides with oil and then season with 1 teaspoon paprika, 3/4 teaspoon sea salt, 1/2 teaspoon garlic powder, 1 teaspoon Italian seasoning, and 1/4 teaspoon black pepper.
- Add all the vegetables to a large-sized bowl and toss with remaining seasonings and 1/4 cup olive oil.
- Arrange vegetables all around the chicken in a single layer.
- Roast for 15 minutes, toss the veggies and roast further until vegetables turn golden brown, for 10 to 15 minutes.
- Remove and serve warm!

Baked Balsamic Chicken Thighs Recipe

Serves: 6 / Preparation time: 5 minutes / Cooking time: 18 minutes

6 cloves garlic, minced

Balsamic glaze (optional)

12 medium (~3 lbs.) boneless skinless chicken thighs

1/4 teaspoon black pepper

1/4 cup olive oil

1 teaspoon sea salt

1/4 cup balsamic vinegar

1 teaspoon Italian seasoning

- Whisk together all the ingredients in a large-sized bowl except for chicken.
- Add in chicken and coat with marinade on all sides.
- Refrigerate for an hour or up to 2 days.
- After taking it out from the refrigerator, preheat your oven to a temperature of 425 ° F (218°C).
- Line one extra-large baking sheet with parchment paper.
- Arrange chicken onto the lined sheet(s), each with some gap. Do not overlap.
- Bake in a preheated oven until chicken is cooked through or until an internal temperature reaches up to 165°F. It will take about 18 to 20 minutes.
- Once done, let the chicken cool and then drizzle with balsamic glaze.
- Too Yum!

Mexican Cheese And Chicken Stuffed Poblano Peppers

Serves: 6 / Preparation time: 5 minutes / Cooking time: 20 minutes

1 (14.5-oz.) can diced tomatoes (not drained)

Cilantro, for topping (optional)

3 large poblano peppers, cut in half and seeds removed

3/4 cup cheddar cheese, shredded

1 tablespoon butter

3 oz. cream cheese, cubed

2 cloves garlic, minced

2 tablespoons taco seasoning

2 cups chicken, shredded

- Preheat your oven to a temperature of 350°F (176°C).
- Place peppers onto a lined baking sheet and keep it aside.
- Melt butter in a skillet and sauté garlic for 30 seconds, stirring frequently.
- Add in diced tomatoes with liquid, 2 cups of shredded chicken, and 2 tablespoons taco seasoning.
- Bring everything to a boil, then turn down the heat and simmer until extra liquid is absorbed, for 3 to 5 minutes.
- Next, stir in cream cheese until smooth and melted.
- Fill poblano peppers with the prepared filling mixture and place them back onto a baking sheet so that the open side remains up. Sprinkle about 2 tablespoons of cheese over each pepper half.
- Bake in a preheated oven until cheese is melted, for about 15 to 20 minutes.
- Once done, finish with a garnish of fresh cilantro.

Creamy Dijon Mustard Chicken Recipe

Serves: 4 / Preparation time: 5 minutes / Cooking time: 15 minutes

2 cloves garlic, minced

2 tablespoons whole-grain Dijon mustard

4 (8-oz.) chicken breasts

1 tablespoon fresh thyme

1/2 teaspoon sea salt

2/3 cup heavy cream

1/4 teaspoon black pepper

1/2 cup chicken broth

2 tablespoons olive oil, divided

- Season both sides of chicken breasts with pepper and salt.
- Preheat a tablespoon of oil in a cast-iron skillet and add in chicken. Cook each side for 4 to 8 minutes, until golden brown on all sides. Once done, remove it from a plate and cover it to keep warm.
- Add remaining oil to the same pan and sauté garlic until fragrant for a minute.
- Next, stir in 1/2 cup chicken broth, removing bits stuck to the bottom, if any.
- Raise the heat and simmer until liquid is reduced by half. It will take 3 to 5 minutes.
- Add in 1 tablespoon fresh thyme and 2/3 cup heavy cream and continue simmering for a few minutes, scraping the bottom of the pan.
- Once the sauce thickens, stir in 2 tablespoons of whole-grain Dijon mustard and turn the flame off.
- Pour sauce over chicken and serve immediately!

Easy Tandoori Chicken Recipe In The Oven

Serves: 4 / Preparation time: 10 minutes / Cooking time: 35 minutes

Chicken:

4 whole Chicken legs, thighs, and drumsticks connected

For Marinade:

1 pinch black pepper

1 cup full-fat Greek yogurt

1 pinch sea salt

1 tablespoon lime juice

1/2 teaspoon cayenne pepper

1 clove garlic, minced

1/2 teaspoon ground ginger

1 tablespoon garam masala

For Frying:

2 tablespoons olive oil

- Add all the marinade ingredients to a large-sized bowl and mix well.
- Add in chicken and stir until all sides are coated with the marinade. Wrap your bowl with plastic and refrigerate for an hour or two.
- After taking it out from the refrigerator, preheat your oven to a temperature of 400 °F (204°C).
- Preheat oil in a cast iron pan and add in chicken legs. Cook each side for 5 minutes, until chicken is browned on all sides.
- Then place this pan inside a preheated oven and cook for another 25 to 35 minutes. The time may vary, depending upon the thickness of the chicken.
- Once done, take it out & serve warm!

Seafood

Cod Scrambled Eggs

Serves: 2 / Preparation time: 5 minutes / Cooking time: 25 minutes

1 tablespoon olive oil, divided

1/4 teaspoon sea salt

1/2 cup leeks, thinly sliced

1/2 tablespoon water

6 Oz. (1 large fillet) fresh cod

4 large eggs

Seasoning salt

- Add sliced leeks to a bowl and cover with cold water. Leave until required.
- Pat the cod dry and season both of its sides with seasoning salt.
- Add a teaspoon of oil to a nonstick pan and preheat over medium-high heat. Cook each side of the cod fillet for 2 to 3 minutes, until golden brown.
- Reduce the flame and break the fillet into large chunks.
- Again add half a teaspoon of oil to the same pan.
- Drain the thinly sliced leeks and dry them using clean paper kitchen towels. Add to the pan and cook for 2 to 3 minutes, until softened.
- Turn off the flame leave the pan for 5 minutes.
- In the meantime, whisk together 4 eggs and 1/2 tablespoon water until slightly frothy.
- Put the pan on the stove again and add in a remaining half tablespoon of oil—Preheat over low flame for a minute or two.
- Pour egg mixture into the pan without disturbing anything. Once the bottom begins to set, whisk and again do not touch until the bottom is set. Continue repeating until eggs are cooked about 75%.
- Once done, add in salt and whisk. Repeat this process 1 to 2 times until eggs are cooked about 90%.
- Turn the flame off and whisk until eggs are soft and set.

- Serve delicious keto Mediterranean cod scrambled eggs right away!

Crab Cakes

Serves: 8 crab cakes / Preparation time: 10 minutes / Cooking time: 15 minutes

2 teaspoons coconut aminos

2 tablespoons avocado oil for frying

8 oz. blue crab meat, drained (there should be no cartilage or shells in the meat)

2 teaspoons Old Bay seasoning

2 tablespoons mayonnaise

2 tablespoons coconut flour

1 teaspoon Dijon mustard

2 tablespoons parsley, freshly chopped

1 tablespoon fresh lemon juice

- Add crab meat to a small-sized bowl.
- Take another bowl and whisk together 1 teaspoon coconut aminos, 1 teaspoon Dijon mustard, 2 tablespoons mayonnaise, and 1 tablespoon fresh lemon juice., until smooth.
- In a third bowl, combine together 2 tablespoons coconut flour, 2 tablespoons freshly chopped parsley, and 2 teaspoons Old Bay seasoning.
- Fold mayonnaise mixture into a bowl with crab meat until combined.
- Then add in dry ingredients and mix well. Make sure to not shred or break up the crab a lot. Shape into 8 small cakes, 2-inch diameter each.
- Preheat coconut oil in a nonstick pan.
- Place crab cakes carefully into a pan with hot oil and cook each side for 2 to 3 minutes, until nicely golden brown.
- Once done, remove to a plate lined with paper towel and serve immediately with roasted red pepper sauce and lemon wedges.

Air Fryer Salmon

Serves: 2 / Preparation time: 2 minutes / Cooking time: 10 minutes

8 oz. (2 fillets each 4 oz.)Wild-caught salmon

Sea salt

1 teaspoon olive oil

- Rub salmon fillets with oil on all sides and then sprinkle with salt.
- Place into an air fryer basket and cook for about 6 to 8 minutes at 400°F (204 °C), or until an internal temperature of fillet reaches up to a temperature of 120 degrees F (48.889°C). You can check it with an instant-read thermometer. Cooking time may vary depending upon the thickness of the fillet.
- Once done, leave for 5 to 10 minutes and then serve!

Air Fryer Mahi Mahi With Lime Butter

Serves: 4 / Preparation time: 5 minutes / Cooking time: 10 minutes

1/2 tablespoon olive oil

Salt

1 lb. (about 4 fillets) Mahi Mahi fillets

3/4 teaspoon Old Bay seasoning

For The Lime Butter:

1/4 teaspoon lime zest, packed

Pinch of salt

2 tablespoons butter, softened to room temperature

1/2 teaspoon fresh lime juice plus more for garnish

- Brush fish with oil on all sides and season with some salt and bay seasoning.
- Place fish into a mesh air fryer basket and cook for about 7 to 9 minutes at 400°F (204°C). Time may vary depending upon the thickness of fish fillets. The internal temperature of fish should be about 140°F (62°C).
- Once done, remove from air fryer and let it stand for 10 minutes, covered.
- In the meantime, mix together lime butter ingredients in a small-sized bowl.
- Serve warm fish with lime butter sauce.
- Bon appetite!

Mediterranean Salmon

Serves: 4 / Preparation time: 8 minutes / Cooking time: 30 minutes

1/4 teaspoon dried oregano

Fresh cilantro or parsley

2 lbs. wild salmon

1 whole lemon

1 1/2 tablespoons olive oil

2 tablespoons capers

1 pinch sea salt and pepper, to taste

1/2 cup olives

1 bunch fresh asparagus, trimmed

- Preheat your oven to 350 °F (176 °C).
- Take a baking sheet and line it with foil.
- Brush salmon on with a tablespoon of oil on all sides, and then season with pepper and salt.
- Also, add a splash of lemon juice.
- Bake in a preheated oven for half an hour.
- In the meantime, season trimmed asparagus first with 1/2 tablespoon of olive oil and then with 1/4 teaspoon of dried oregano.
- Once salmon is cooked to half (15 minutes), add asparagus.
- In the meantime, make the salad by combining together capers, olives, and parsley/cilantro. Keep it aside.
- Once salmon is cooked through, top with capers-olives salad.
- Give another splash of lemon juice and serve right away!

15 Minute Garlic Shrimp Zoodles

Serves: 2 / Preparation time: 8 minutes / Cooking time: 7 minutes

Juice and zest of 1 lemon

Salt & pepper, to taste

2 medium zucchini

Red pepper flakes (optional)

3/4 lbs. medium shrimp, peeled & deveined

3-4 cloves garlic, minced

1 tablespoon olive oil

Fresh parsley, chopped

- Preheat a tablespoon of olive oil in a skillet along with juice and zest of 1 lemon. Cook shrimp on each side for a minute.
- Add in red pepper flakes and minced garlic cloves and continue cooking for another minute, stirring occasionally.
- Next, add in zucchini noodles and toss two to three times with tongs until they warm up.
- Season the noodles with pepper and salt to taste.
- Finish with a sprinkle of chopped parsley.

Tuna Stuffed Avocado

Serves: 2 / Preparation time: 15 minutes / Cooking time: 0 minutes

1 (1½ oz.) celery stalk, finely chopped

1 tablespoon fresh chives, finely chopped (optional)

2 (14 oz.) avocados, halved lengthwise, pit removed

Salt and ground black pepper, to taste

5 oz. tuna in water, drained

2¾ tablespoons (1 oz.) red onions, finely chopped

¼ cup mayonnaise or vegan mayonnaise

- Combine together ¼ cup mayonnaise or vegan mayonnaise, finely chopped onion, celery, and tuna in a medium-sized bowl—season with pepper and salt to taste.
- Fill each avocado half with tuna filling and top with a garnish of chives.

Mediterranean Tomato Stew With Calamari

Serves: 2 / Preparation time: 10 minutes / Cooking time: 20 minutes

2 (8 oz.) tomatoes, cut into cubes

Salt and ground black pepper, to taste

3 garlic cloves, minced

½ teaspoon fresh rosemary, chopped

1 (4 oz.) red onion, cut into rings

1 teaspoon fresh dill, chopped

2 tablespoons olive oil

1 teaspoon fresh parsley, chopped

14 oz. (12/3 cups) canned whole tomatoes, peeled

1 lb. squid, cleaned and sliced into rings

- Add oil to a pan and preheat over medium flame.
- Cook garlic and onion together until onion is translucent, stirring often.
- Next, add in canned tomatoes. Fill its can with water, shake a bit and add to the pan. Simmer everything for a few minutes.
- Then add in cubes of fresh tomato and squid slices and continue simmering until squid has cooked through, for another 5 minutes.
- Season with pepper and salt.
- Add chopped herbs to the soup and serve immediately.

Grilled White Fish with Zucchini and Kale Pesto

Serves: 4 / Preparation time: 10 minutes / Cooking time: 15 minutes

For Kale Pesto:

1 garlic clove

½ cup olive oil

3 oz. kale, roughly chopped

¼ teaspoon ground black pepper

3 tablespoons lemon juice or lime juice

½ teaspoon salt

9 tablespoons (2 oz.) walnuts

For Fish And Zucchini:

½ teaspoon salt

¼ teaspoon ground black pepper

1¼ lbs. zucchini, rinsed and thinly sliced

1½ lbs. white fish fillets

1 tablespoon lemon juice

2 tablespoons olive oil

- The process is roughly chopped in a food processor along with garlic, walnuts, and lemon or lime juice until smooth.
- Season with pepper and salt to taste.
- Add 2 tablespoons of olive oil towards the end of processing and set it aside.
- Add zucchini slices to a bowl and season with pepper and salt.
- Add in a tablespoon of lemon juice and 2 tablespoons of olive oil and toss well.
- Season fish with salt on both sides and leave for a few minutes.
- Wipe off excess liquid from fish, if any, and brush with oil.
- Grill/fry each side for a few minutes over medium-high heat.
- Again season with a bit of pepper and serve with pesto and zucchini.

Superfood Salmon Salad Bowl

Serves: 2 / Preparation time: 15 minutes / Cooking time: 8 minutes

For Salmon:

9 oz. salmon, boneless fillets

Salt and pepper, to taste

2 teaspoons avocado oil/olive oil

For Dressing:

1 tablespoon cider vinegar/lemon juice

Salt and pepper, to taste

1 tablespoon capers

1 teaspoon coconut aminos

1 tablespoon Dijon mustard/whole-grain mustard

3 tablespoons olive oil

For Salad:

4 tablespoons (½ oz.) sun-dried tomatoes, chopped

1 tablespoon sunflower seeds

7 oz. cucumber, diced

1 tablespoon pumpkin seeds

2 oz. sugar snap peas, sliced into matchsticks

3 tablespoons fresh dill/parsley/basil/chives, chopped

3 tablespoons (1 oz.) red bell peppers, sliced

5 oz. avocados, diced

3 1/3 tablespoons (1 oz.) olives, pitted and halved

- Season the salmon fillets with pepper and salt.
- Grease a pan with avocado oil and preheat it over medium-high.
- Place salmon in a pan in a way that the skin-side remains down. Cook for 5 to 6 minutes, flip over and continue another side until cooked through for a minute or two.
- Once done, remove from pan. Pull off its skin and flake fillet into chunks.
- To Prepare Dressing: Add all the dressing ingredients to a bowl and mix well.
- To Prepare Salad: Combine together all the salad ingredients in a large-sized bowl except for seeds.
- Add flakes salmon to a salad bowl.

- Fry a tablespoon of each pumpkin seed and sunflower seeds in a pan until golden brown. Once done, let them cool.
- Drizzle with dressing and enjoy a delicious salmon salad bowl.

Mediterranean Fish Bake

Serves: 4 / Preparation time: 10-15 minutes / Cooking time: 15-20 minutes

5 oz. tomatoes sliced

2 tablespoons olive oil

1/4 cup ghee, melted

1 lemon, sliced

2 cloves garlic, minced

4 fillets sea bass

1 eggplant, diced into 1-inch pieces

Pepper, to taste

2 zucchini, sliced

Salt, to taste

1 any color bell pepper, sliced

1/4 cup chopped herbs (basil and oregano)

1 bunch of broccolini florets

1 red onion, sliced

- First, preheat your oven to a temperature of 400° F (204°C).
- In the meantime, combine together garlic with ghee in a small-sized bowl.
- Add all the veggies to a baking tray and sprinkle with chopped herbs, reserving some for garnish.
- Season with pepper, salt, and drizzle with the ghee-garlic mix.
- Bake for about 15 minutes. Once this cooking cycle has been completed, pull out your baking tray and add seasoned fish fillets with pepper and salt to your tastes. Make sure to place it in a way that the skin side of the fish remains up.
- Top with lemon slices and raise your oven temperature to 475°F (246°C)—Bake for about 10 to 12 minutes. To crisp up the skin, you can broil for a minute or two.
- Once done, take out the tray from the oven, discard lemon slices, and drizzle the top of the fish with olive oil.
- Finish with a sprinkle of leftover chopped herbs and serve this delicious meal immediately!

Low Carb Mediterranean Garlic Shrimp

Serves: 4 / Preparation time: 10 minutes / Cooking time: 18 minutes

½ teaspoon ground black pepper

¼ cup fresh parsley or basil, chopped

1 lb. large shrimp, peeled and deveined

¼ cup feta cheese, crumbled

1 tablespoon garlic, minced

1 Roma tomato, diced

2 tablespoons olive oil

2 lemons, juiced

2 tablespoons butter

¼ teaspoon red pepper flakes (optional)

½ teaspoon salt

- First, preheat your oven to a temperature of 400 °F (204°C).
- Add 2 tablespoons of butter to a square pan (8-inch) along with a tablespoon of minced garlic and 2 tablespoons of olive oil. Cook in the oven until garlic sizzles for a few minutes.
- Pat the shrimp dry with a paper towel and season with pepper, salt, and red pepper flakes.
- Add shrimp to a pan with garlic and butter and cook for 5 minutes.
- Once done, take your pan out from the oven and add in diced tomatoes, ¼ cup feta crumbled cheese, diced tomato, and basil or parsley. Drizzle top with lemon juice.
- Bake again until shrimp has cooked through, for about 7 to 10 minutes.

Easy Low Carb Mediterranean Cod

Serves: 4 / Preparation time: 10 minutes / Cooking time: 20 minutes

1 tablespoon parmesan cheese

1 lb. cod or other mild white fish

1 teaspoon anchovy paste

1 cup chicken broth or vegetable broth

1 tablespoon olive oil

20 olives, sliced in half

2 cloves garlic, crushed

1 cup grape tomatoes, sliced in half

4 tablespoons tomato paste

- Preheat olive oil in a pan over medium-high.
- Season cod fillets with pepper and salt and cook in a pan until browned on all sides. It will take a minute or two.
- Remove cod from pan and set aside.
- Reduce the flame and add in 4 tablespoons tomato paste, 1 cup chicken broth or vegetable broth, and 1 teaspoon anchovy paste. Whisk well and then add in sliced olives, crushed garlic cloves, and tomato halves.
- Simmer at low for about 5 minutes. Add in cod and continue cooking for another 5 minutes, covered.
- Serve over zucchini noodles or cauliflower rice.

Low Carb Almond Crusted Cod

Serves: 4 / Preparation time: 15 minutes / Cooking time: 7 minutes

1 tablespoon dill

4 teaspoons Dijon mustard

4 filets cod or other white fish

1 teaspoon chili spice (optional)

1 lemon, zested and juiced

Salt & pepper, to taste

1/2 cup almonds, crushed

1 tablespoon olive oil

- First, preheat your oven to 400°F (204°C).

- Take a baking sheet and line it with parchment paper.

- Pat the cod fillets dry with clean paper towels to drain water. Place these fillets onto a prepared baking sheet.

- In a small-sized bowl, combine together lemon juice, lemon zest, oil, almonds, pepper, salt, and chili spice.

- Spread both sides of the cod fillet with Dijon mustard.

- Divide almond-chili mixture among all fillets, pressing into the mustard evenly using your hands.

- Bake fish in a preheated oven for about 7 minutes, or until fillets have cooked through and opaque at the thickest part. Serve with slices of lemon and green vegetables.

Keto Salmon With Pesto And Spinach

Serves: 4 / Preparation time: 5 minutes / Cooking time: 20 minutes

¾ cup (2 oz.) Parmesan cheese, shredded

Salt and pepper

1½ lbs. salmon, boneless fillets

1 oz. butter or olive oil

1 cup mayonnaise/sour cream/ vegan mayonnaise

1 lb. (15 cups) fresh spinach

1 tablespoon green pesto or red pesto

- First, preheat your oven to 400°F (204°C).
- Take a baking dish and grease it with half of butter or oil.
- Place salmon fillets in a prepared dish in a way that the skin side remains down.
- Season the fillets with pepper and salt.
- Combine together a cup of mayonnaise, ¾ cup shredded parmesan, and a tablespoon of green or red pesto. Spread this mixture over fillets.
- Place baking dish on the center rack and bake for about 20 to 30 minutes. Time may vary depending upon the thickness of fillets.
- In the meantime, preheat leftover oil or butter in a large pan and sauté spinach until wilted for about 2 minutes.
- Season with pepper and salt to taste.
- Serve baked salmon with spinach and enjoy your meal!

Salmon with a Maple Walnut Crusted

Serves: 4 / Preparation time: 9 minutes / Cooking time: 10 minutes

4 (6 oz.) salmon fillets

Sprinkle of salt and pepper

2 tablespoon olive oil

For Maple Walnut Crust

1/2 teaspoon cracked black pepper

1 tablespoon apple cider vinegar

3 tablespoon pure maple syrup

1 teaspoon coconut aminos

1/2 teaspoon onion powder

1/2 cup finely chopped walnuts

1/2 teaspoon chipotle powder

1 teaspoon smoked paprika

- In a small mixing bowl, add all of the Maple Walnut Crust ingredients and stir until thoroughly blended.

- Place the salmon fillets on a platter and spoon the sauce over each one, spreading it out as evenly as possible. Allow 2 to 3 hours in the refrigerator, uncovered.

- Preheat the oven to 425°F.

- In a large oven-safe skillet, heat the oil. When the pan is nice and hot, add the fish pieces and cook them for about 2 minutes, or until the skin is lovely and crispy.

- Place the pan in the oven and cook the fish for another 5-8 minutes, depending on desired doneness and fillet thickness. Turn the flame off and whisk until eggs are soft and set.

Roasted Salmon with Parmesan Dill Crust

Serves: 2 / Preparation time: 2 minutes / Cooking time: 10 minutes

¼ cup mayonnaise

2 pieces of salmon

1 tablespoon dill weed

1 tablespoon ground mustard

¼ cup grated parmesan cheese

- Preheat the oven to 450°F (232 °C).
- Combine together all the ingredients in a medium-sized bowl except for salmon.
- Place salmon onto a baking sheet lined with foil.
- Top each salmon with half of the prepared mixture.
- Roast for 10 minutes in a preheated oven or until fish flakes easily using a fork.
- Serve warm!

Fattoush salad with Tilapia

Serves: 4 / Preparation time: 9 minutes / Cooking time: 15 minutes

For Tilapia Fillets:

4 Fresh Tilapia fillets

1 ½ tablespoon olive oil

2 teaspoon za'atar

½ teaspoon sumac

¼ teaspoon salt

1 large head romaine chopped

1 tablespoon fresh mint diced

1 cup grape tomatoes halved

1 cucumber, diced

½ cup feta

2 pita rounds, sliced into triangles

For Chickpea Mix

1 ½ cups chickpeas

1 shallot, sliced thinly

1 ½ tablespoon olive oil

1 tablespoon za'atar

1 teaspoon sumac

¼ teaspoon salt

For Salad Dressing

¼ cup extra virgin olive oil

2 tablespoon honey

1 lemon, zest, and juiced

Salt and pepper to taste1 teaspoon olive oil

- Preheat the oven to 400°F (204 °).
- Lay fillets on a baking sheet and cover with 2 teaspoons of za'atar, ½ tablespoon of olive oil, ¼ teaspoon of salt, and ½ teaspoon of sumac.
- Arrange shallots and chickpeas onto a separate baking sheet and drizzle with 1 ½ tablespoon of olive oil. Season the veggies with ¼ teaspoon of salt, 1 teaspoon of sumac, and a tablespoon of za'atar. Toss well.
- Put both baking trays inside a preheated oven for 10 minutes.
- Once done, remove the tilapia fillets tray from the oven and keep it aside.
- Give a toss to shallots and chickpeas and bake for another 5 minutes.

- Lay pita triangles onto a baking sheet and bake until the bottom is slightly crispy and browned. It may take 5 to 7 minutes.
- In the meantime, add all the dressing ingredients to a jar and shake vigorously until combined.
- Combine together diced cucumber, a cup of halved grape tomatoes, chopped romaine, a tablespoon of diced mint, and ½ cup feta in a large-sized bowl.
- Once done with shallots and chickpeas, remove them from the oven and transfer them to a bowl with cucumber and tomatoes. Toss with dressing.
- Divide salad among serving platters and top each with a Tilapia fillet and toasted pita points.

Spicy Fish Stew

Serves: 4 / Preparation time: 10 minutes / Cooking time: 20 minutes

1 teaspoon Paprika

1 medium red pepper

1 medium lime, juiced

1 medium Onion

2 cloves Garlic

15 ounces coconut milk (canned)

1 pound wild-caught white fish

2 cups Chicken Bone Broth

1 medium jalapeno pepper (deseeded)

1 medium yellow pepper

1 teaspoon Sea Salt

1/4 teaspoon Black Pepper

2 cups chopped tomatoes

Optional garnishes:

Additional lime wedges

Chopped fresh cilantro

- Add fish to a large-sized bowl and toss with lime juice. Keep the bowl aside.
- Preheat oil in a pan and sauté onions and peppers for a few minutes until onions are translucent, stirring often.
- Next, stir in garlic for 30 seconds.
- Stir in tomatoes, spices, and broth. Bring everything to a boil, and then add in fish and coconut milk.
- Once boiled, turn the heat down and simmer for about 10 minutes, covered.
- Garnish with cilantro and serve with lime wedges.
- Wow, this keto Mediterranean meal is so delicious!

Shrimp boil

Serves: 5 / Preparation time: 15 minutes / Cooking time: 25 minutes

1 Link Andouille sausage, cut into slices

3 cup Water

½ medium onion, cut into wedges

1 pound Shrimp peeled, deveined, and tails off

1 small yellow squash, sliced

¼ cup Old Bay seasoning

Chopped parsley for garnish

4 teaspoon minced garlic

Salt and pepper to taste

3 cup cauliflower florets

2 cup Chicken broth

3 tablespoon melted butter

- Add chicken broth to a large pot along with Old Bay seasoning, onion, water, and garlic. Bring everything to a boil.
- Add in pepper, salt, and cauliflower and continue boiling for another 3 minutes.
- Next, add in sausage, shrimp, and squash. Mix well, boil, put on the lid, and then cook until shrimp is cooked through, for 5 to 10 minutes.
- Once done, drain the liquid and transfer the mixture to a serving bowl.
- Finish with a drizzle of butter and sprinkle of parsley.

Tuna casserole

Serves: 6 / Preparation time: 15 minutes / Cooking time: 40 minutes

1/2 cup sliced green onions

3 cups roasted cauliflower florets

1 tablespoon basil, chopped.

2 teaspoons of Dijon mustard

2 cans (6.5 oz.) tuna, salmon, crab, or shrimp

1/4 teaspoon of pepper

1/2 cup mayonnaise

1 cup shredded jack cheese

1/4 cup pork rind panko

1/2 cup chopped celery

1 small zucchini, very thinly sliced

1/2 cup sour cream

1/2 teaspoon of salt

- Preheat the oven to 350°F (176°C).
- Drain the tuna well or any other seafood of your choice. Keep it aside.
- Mix together mayonnaise, tuna, sour cream, cauliflower, pepper, mustard, salt, green onions, herbs, and celery in a large-sized bowl.
- Spoon half of the mixture into a buttered baking dish (1-1/2 quart).
- Layer the mixture with half of each zucchini and cheese.
- Cover with remaining mayonnaise mixture followed by zucchini and cheese on top.
- Sprinkle top with pork rind panko and bake in a preheated oven until cheese is bubbly, for about 40 minutes.
- Garnish with fresh herbs and enjoy!

Baked Salmon with Mayo

Serves: 4 / Preparation time: 4 minutes / Cooking time: 14 minutes

2 tablespoons parmesan cheese, grated

4 salmon fillets

2 tablespoons pork panko

2 teaspoons Italian seasoning

4 tablespoons mayonnaise

Pinch of pepper

- Preheat the oven to 375°F (190°C).
- Pat the salmon fillets dry using a clean paper towel and place them onto a parchment-lined baking sheet.
- Spread top of each fillet with mayonnaise and sprinkle with panko, grated cheese, Italian seasoning, and finally with pepper.
- Bake in a preheated oven until fish flakes easily using a fork. It may take 12 to 14 minutes.
- Serve immediately.

Keto Mediterranean Battered Fish

Serves: 4 / Preparation time: 9 minutes / Cooking time: 15 minutes

1/4 cup Unflavored Protein Powder

1/4 cup Sparkling Water chilled

1.7 lbs. Whitefish, cut into evenly sized pieces

2/3 cup Almond Flour

2 teaspoons Baking Powder

1/2 teaspoon salt

Lemon wedges to serve

1/4 cup Keto Tartar Sauce

2 large Eggs

- Place fish pieces in a tray and season with ¼ teaspoon of salt.
- Add remaining salt to a separate bowl and mix with protein powder, almond flour, and baking powder.
- Gently whisk in water and eggs until incorporated. Leave for 10 minutes.
- Heat the deep fryer to 355°F (179°C).
- Pat the fish pieces dry using a clean paper towel.
- Now start dipping fish pieces, one by one, into the batter, shaking off excess and then dropping into the hot oil.
- Do this in batches, if required.
- Flip over the fish pieces and cook another side until golden brown. It will take around 5 to 8 minutes.
- Once done with all, drain in dryer basket and let it sit for 5 to 10 minutes.
- Enjoy a delicious keto battered dish with fresh lemon and keto tartar sauce.

Creamy Sardine Salad

Serves: 4 / Preparation time: 4 minutes / Cooking time: 0 minutes

1 tablespoon paleo mayonnaise

1 (3.2 oz.) can sardine, drained

Sea salt and pepper, to taste

1 teaspoon fresh lemon juice

1/4 small red onion, finely diced

Keto bread to serve (optional)

- Combine together mayonnaise, sardines, lemon juice, and diced red onion in a large-sized bowl. Mash using a fork.
- Season the sardine mixture with pepper and salt according to your preferences.
- Serve with bell pepper halves, leafy salad bowls, or crunchy vegetables.

Low carb clam chowder

Serves: 12 / Preparation time: 5 minutes / Cooking time: 8-9 minutes

2 ribs celery, diced

¼ cup chicken stock

1 medium onion, chopped

1 teaspoon garlic powder

1 pound thick-cut bacon, cooked crisp and crumbled

4 cloves garlic, minced

1 shallot, thinly sliced

1 teaspoon black pepper

1 ½ cups heavy cream

1 small leek, cleaned, trimmed, and sliced

2 teaspoon sea salt

1 teaspoon dried thyme

2 tablespoons butter

3 (10 oz.) cans whole baby clams, drained

2 cups clam juice

8 oz. cream cheese, softened

- Heat the slow cooker over a low setting.
- Add garlic to slow cooker along with butter, chicken stock, celery, pepper, salt, onions, leek, and shallot.
- Cook for an hour on low, covered.
- Next, add in clam juice, clams, cooked and crumbled bacon, thyme, heavy cream, cream cheese, and garlic powder.
- Mix well until all ingredients are incorporated, and no clumps are left.
- Cook for 6 to 8 hours, covered.

Lemon garlic steam clams

Serves: 2 / Preparation time: 23 minutes / Cooking time: 5 minutes

½ lemon, juiced

2 tablespoons chopped parsley

2 pounds fresh clams

1 small onion, diced

1 cup chicken stock

½ teaspoon crushed red pepper flakes

3 cloves garlic, minced

2 tablespoons grass-fed butter

½ teaspoon dried thyme

½ teaspoon sea salt

- Add clams to a pot with cold, salted water and soak for 20 minutes.
- Combine together all the remaining ingredients in a large pot and bring to a boil over medium flame. Cook for about 3 to 5 minutes or until clams has opened, covered.
- Remove everything to a serving bowl and garnish with extra lemon and parsley.

Broiled Oyster with Spicy Sauce

Serves: 2 / Preparation time: 9 minutes / Cooking time: 12 minutes

12 oysters shucked

1 tablespoon olive oil

7-8 basil leaves fresh

⅛ teaspoon salt

1 tablespoon garlic chili paste

- Combine together olive oil, garlic chili paste, and salt in a medium-sized bowl.
- Add in oysters and mix well until coated with sauce.
- Lay basil leaves in an oven-safe baking dish and pours over oysters and sauce mixture, spreading evenly.
- Turn on the broiler to high.
- Place oven-safe dish within a few inches from broiler, on the top rack.
- Broil on high for just 2 to 3 minutes.
- Serve warm!

Crab Stuffed Mushrooms

Serves: 5 / Preparation time: 20 minutes / Cooking time: 30 minutes

1 tablespoon Dijon mustard

3 cloves garlic, minced

6 ounces cream cheese, softened

6 strips bacon, cooked crisp and crumbled

12 oz. fresh lump crab meat

¼ cup sour cream

1 pound large cremini mushrooms, cleaned and de-stemmed

Sea salt and pepper, to taste

3 green onions, chopped

½ cup shredded Parmesan cheese

⅓ cup shredded sharp cheddar cheese

- Preheat the oven to 400 °F (204 °C)
- Bake mushroom caps in a parchment-lined rimmed baking sheet for 10 minutes.
- Pour out the excess moisture from mushroom caps, if any.
- Add remaining ingredients to a medium-sized bowl except for parmesan cheese and combine well until incorporated.
- Stuff each mushroom cap with crab filling mixture and bake for about 10 minutes.
- Take the dish out of the oven and top each with cheese.
- Bake further until cheese is golden brown, for 5 to 10 minutes.

Steamed Clams with Basil Butter

Serves: 4 / Preparation time: 3 minutes / Cooking time: 10 minutes

½ cup chicken broth

1 clove garlic minced

1 pound steamer-sized clams in shell small

10 fresh basil leaves

- Add butter to a saucepan and melt over medium flame.
- Once melted, add broth, basil leaves, and minced garlic. Bring everything to a boil.
- Add in clams and mix well. Put on the tight-fitting lid and steam for about 7 to 8 minutes.
- While steaming, shake the pan carefully once or twice.
- Put the lid off. If the sauce is too much thin, continue cooking until it reaches your desired consistency.
- You can add an additional tablespoon of butter at this step if desired.
- Turn the heat off once done.
- Discard non-opened clams and serve right away!

Crab legs

Serves: 2 / Preparation time: 10 minutes / Cooking time: 5 minutes

1 lb. king crab legs

1/2 tablespoon lemon juice

3 cloves garlic, minced

Lemon slices

4 tablespoons salted butter, melted

1 tablespoon chopped parsley

- Preheat the oven to 375°F (190°C).
- If using frozen crab legs, thaw them first.
- Cut legs into halves and arrange them on a tray or baking sheet evenly.
- Add butter to a microwave-safe bowl and heat for 30 seconds.
- Then stir in parsley, garlic, and lemon juice.
- Spread this mixture over crab legs, leaving some amount for dipping.
- Bake in a preheated oven until crab legs are heated through, for about 5 minutes.
- Serve warm with lemon slices and remaining butter.
- Drizzle with lemon juice and serve immediately!

Low Carb Soft Shell Crab

Serves: 2 / Preparation time: 8 minutes / Cooking time: 10 minutes

4 tablespoons Carolina BBQ sauce

8 soft shell crabs (2 packages)

2 eggs, beaten

½ cup powdered parmesan

- Add ½ cup lard or tallow to a cast-iron skillet and preheat over medium flame.
- Pat dry the crab with a clean paper towel.
- Add powdered parmesan to a large shallow dish.
- Take another shallow dish and crack eggs into it. Beat well.
- First, dip the crab into beaten eggs and then coat with powdered parmesan on all sides.
- Drop crabs, 3 to 4 at a time, into oil and cook for 4 to 5 minutes, flipping once in between.
- Repeat the same process with leftover carbs.
- Serve warm with delicious Carolina BBQ sauce.

Cajun Trinity Keto Crab Cakes

Serves: 8 crab cakes / Preparation time: 15 minutes / Cooking time: 20 minutes

2 tablespoons mayonnaise

2 tablespoons olive oil

2 tablespoons butter

1 lb. lump crabmeat, picked clean of shells

1 large rib celery, chopped

½ cup crushed pork rinds

½ cup mixed bell pepper, chopped

½ cup Parmesan cheese, grated

1 shallot, chopped

1 teaspoon hot sauce

2 cloves garlic, minced

1 teaspoon spicy brown mustard

Sea salt and black pepper, to taste

1 tablespoon Worcestershire sauce

1 large egg

- Preheat butter in a sauté pan.
- Add in ½ cup mixed chopped bell pepper, black pepper, salt, 2 minced cloves of garlic, chopped shallot, and celery. Sauté veggies for 10 minutes until softened and translucent.
- Combine together 1 tablespoon Worcestershire sauce, 1 teaspoon spicy brown mustard, 2 tablespoons mayonnaise, 1 teaspoon hot sauce, and egg in a medium-sized bowl.
- Add in sautéed veggies and combine well.
- Next, mix in ½ cup crushed pork rinds and ½ cup grated parmesan cheese.
- Fold crab into this mixture and shape into 8 patties (must be of equal size).
- Place crab patties onto a parchment-lined baking sheet and refrigerate for an hour or two.
- Fry patties in oil until both sides are crispy and brown, flipping just one time in between.

Cheese And Seafood-Stuffed Mushrooms

Serves: 36 pieces / Preparation time: 10 minutes / Cooking time: 20 minutes

1/2 cup sharp cheddar cheese, grated

36 white button mushrooms, stems removed

6 oz. cream cheese, at room temperature

1/4 teaspoon garlic powder

1/4 cup paleo mayo

1 teaspoon Frank's Red Hot (optional)

1 - 4.25 oz. can crab meat, drained

1 tablespoon fresh parsley, chopped

1 cup cooked shrimp, finely chopped

1 teaspoon Dijon mustard

1/4 cup parmesan cheese, grated

- Line a baking sheet (13" x 18") with parchment paper.
- Add all the ingredients to a bowl except for mushrooms and mix well until combined.
- Press the filling into the mushroom's cavities gently, creating a small mound on top of each.
- Place mushrooms onto a lined sheet and refrigerate for half an hour.
- Preheat your oven to a temperature of 375°F (190°C).
- Bake mushrooms until tops turn golden brown, for around 20 minutes.
- Once done, take mushrooms out of the oven and leave for 5 minutes.
- Finish with a garnish of chopped parsley.

Crabbed Stuffed Avocado with Lime

Serves: 2 / Preparation time: 10 minutes / Cooking time: 10 minutes

¼ teaspoon fine sea salt

Dash hot sauce or sriracha (optional)

¼ cup avocado oil mayonnaise

Lime wedges, for serving

3 tablespoon p+ 1 teaspoon fresh lime juice, divided

1 ripe California Avocado, halved and pitted

2 tablespoon onion, diced

1 (6- oz.) can crab meat

2 tablespoon fresh cilantro, chopped

Ground pepper, to taste

½ teaspoon ground cumin

- Combine together 3 tablespoon lime juice, ¼ cup avocado oil mayonnaise, ½ teaspoon ground cumin, ¼ teaspoon fine sea salt, pepper, 2 tablespoons fresh chopped cilantro, and 2 tablespoons diced onion in a medium-sized bowl.
- Gently fold in crabmeat.
- Adjust seasonings to your preferences.
- To prevent browning, brush avocado halves with leftover lime juice.
- Place avocado halves onto a plate, cut side up.
- Fill each avocado half with crab salad.
- Drizzle with hot sauce and serve with lime wedges.

Salmon Meatballs

Serves: 16 salmon balls / Preparation time: 10 minutes / Cooking time: 15 minutes

For The Meatballs:

1 teaspoon Worcestershire sauce

1/8 teaspoon black pepper

16 oz. fresh, raw salmon

1/4 teaspoon salt

4 oz. smoked salmon (not lox style), skin and bones removed

1/2 teaspoon garlic powder

1 egg

1 teaspoon chives (or scallions), chopped

1/4 cup almond flour

For The Tartar Sauce:

1/4 cup sour cream

1 tablespoon capers, drained & chopped

1/4 cup mayonnaise

1/2 teaspoon caper brine from the jar

1 tablespoon fresh dill, roughly chopped

2 tablespoons dill pickles or cornichons, chopped

For The Onions:

2 tablespoons fresh lemon juice

1/4 cup red onion, sliced

- For The Onions: Combine together 1/4 cup thinly sliced red onion and 2 tablespoons fresh lemon juice in a small-sized bowl. Refrigerate until ready to serve, covered.
- For The Tartar Sauce: Add all the sauce ingredients to a small-sized bowl and mix well. Chill the sauce until ready to serve.
- For The Meatballs: Dice salmon into small pieces and combine them with the remaining meatball ingredients. Shape into 16 meatballs.
- Fry in little oil, each side for 2 minutes, until golden brown.
- Garnish with lemon wedges and arugula.
- Serve right away!

Salmon In Foil Packets With Pesto

Serves: 4 / Preparation time: 5 minutes / Cooking time: 15 minutes

1/8 teaspoon ground black pepper

1/4 cup prepared basil pesto

4 (4 oz. each) salmon fillets

1/2 cup dry white wine

2 tablespoons olive oil

20 cherry tomatoes

1/2 teaspoon kosher salt

Optional cauliflower rice for serving

- Place salmon onto a large-sized tin foil sheet.
- Season the salmon with pepper and salt on all sides, and then drizzle with oil.
- Place tomatoes around fillets, folding up the foil edges around it so that an inch rim is created to trap the moisture inside.
- Pour wine around salmon and tomatoes.
- Fold extra foil over the salmon packet, crimping lightly to create a sealed package.
- Cook fillets on a preheated grill at 400°F (204°C) for 10 minutes over indirect heat.
- Once done, remove from grill and keep warm.
- Then lift up the foil and brush the top of fillets with pesto.
- Serve with cauliflower rice, if desired.

Ginger Sesame Glazed Salmon

Serves: 2 / Preparation time: 10 minutes / Cooking time: 15 minutes

1 teaspoon ginger, minced

2 tablespoons white wine

10 oz. salmon filet

1 tablespoon sugar-free ketchup

2 tablespoons soy sauce

1 tablespoon red boat fish sauce

2 teaspoons sesame oil

2 teaspoons garlic, minced

1 tablespoon rice vinegar

- Add all the ingredients to a small Tupperware container except for white wine, ketchup, and sesame oil—marinade for 10 to 15 minutes.
- Preheat sesame oil in a pan and place fish, skin-side down.
- Cook each side for 3 to 4 minutes or until done. Time may vary, depending upon the thickness of fish.
- Add in marinate and bring to a boil after flipping the fish.
- Once done, turn off the flame, and add in white wine and ketchup. Simmer for just 5 minutes, and then serve warm!

Salmon With Garlicky Black Pepper

Serves: 6 / Preparation time: 5 minutes / Cooking time: 20 minutes

4 packages Bumble Bee SuperFresh Frozen Salmon fillets

Egg Free Lemon Aioli:

¼ cup lemon juice

2 cloves garlic, minced

½ cup vegan mayo or organic mayonnaise

1 teaspoon lemon zest

¼ cup extra virgin olive oil

Parsley, freshly chopped (optional)

Lemon wedges (optional)

- Preheat your oven as per the instructions mentioned in the package.
- Place each fillet in a parchment package, fold up and place onto a baking sheet.
- Bake in a preheated oven for 20 minutes.
- Meanwhile, prepare egg-free lemon aioli by whisking all the ingredients mentioned under this heading.
- Once fillets are done, carefully remove them from the oven and open the parchment paper.
- Top each baked fillet with an oz. of sauce followed by chopped parsley on top.
- Drizzle with lemon juice, if needed.

Keto Bacon Wrapped Salmon With Pesto

Serves: 1 / Preparation time: 5 minutes / Cooking time: 15 minutes

6 oz. salmon fillet   1 slice bacon

2 tablespoons pesto

- Place bacon onto a flat, clean surface.
- Place fillet across bacon and tightly roll up, securing with a wooden skewer.
- Add 1 to 2 tablespoons of pesto in the center.
- Place bacon-wrapped salmon in a pan and fry until cooked through, for approximately 10 to 12 minutes, covered.
- Alternatively, bake salmon for 15 minutes on a lined baking tray in the oven at 350 degrees F (176.667°C).

Grilled Salmon With Creamy Pesto Sauce

Serves: 4 / Preparation time: 15 minutes / Cooking time: 10 minutes

Salt and freshly ground black pepper

3 tablespoons pesto + additional for serving

4 - 6 (6 oz.) salmon fillets, skin on or skinless

1/4 cup milk

Olive oil, for brushing salmon and grill

4 oz. cream cheese, diced into small cubes

- Preheat grill to about 425°F (218°C) over medium heat.
- Brush a tablespoon of olive oil on both sides of salmon, and then season with pepper and salt.
- After brushing the grill grates with oil, grill salmon until your desired doneness, 3 minutes per side (grill skin side up first if using skin-on salmon).
- In the meantime, add 1/4 cup milk and cream cheese to a saucepan and cook for a minute or two, stirring frequently. Turn off the flame and stir in pesto.
- Serve delicious warm salmon with yummy creamy pesto sauce.

Grilled Salmon Cucumber Salad

Serves: 2 / Preparation time: 5 minutes / Cooking time: 10 minutes

2 cups cucumber, chopped

1 tablespoon extra-virgin olive oil

Dash salt and pepper

1 Atlantic salmon fillet around 0.42 kg, skin removed

1/2 red onion, chopped

2 tablespoons seafood seasoning blend

1 cup cherry tomatoes, chopped

- Cut salmon into 2 to 4 pieces and place in a frying pan.
- Turn on the flame and season with some of the seafood seasonings over fillets. Drizzle with olive oil.
- Cook for 4 minutes, flip over and season another side with remaining seasoning. Cook for another 4 minutes.
- Add chopped tomatoes, cucumber, and onion to a bowl and toss with pepper, salt, and olive oil.
- Once salmon is cooled enough to handle, cut into strips and place on top of the salad.
- Serve and enjoy!

Cajun Salmon Patties

Serves: 2 patties / Preparation time: 10 minutes / Cooking time: 15 minutes

3 tablespoons Hidden Valley Ranch Cilantro Lime dressing

2 tablespoons avocado oil for frying

14 oz. can pink salmon, drained with bones removed

1 teaspoon Cajun seasoning

2 oz. smoked salmon, roughly chopped (nova or lox style),

2 tablespoons fresh parsley, chopped

1 egg

1/3 cup almond flour

- Whisk together Cilantro Lime dressing and egg in a medium-sized bowl.
- Stir in parsley, salmon, Cajun seasoning, and almond flour until combined.
- Shape into 8 patties (2.5 inches each).
- Preheat oil in a nonstick pan.
- Cook 4 patties at a time, each side for 2 minutes or until golden brown.
- Once done, remove to a plate lined with a paper towel.
- Serve with hidden valley ranch cilantro lime dressing and garnish with lemon wedges.

Easy Keto Salmon Cakes

Serves: 2 / Preparation time: 10 minutes / Cooking time: 15 minutes

Salmon Cakes:

2 tablespoons red onion, finely diced

1 tablespoon avocado oil

Two (5 oz.) pouches of pink salmon

Salt and pepper, to taste

1 egg

1/4 teaspoon chili powder

1/4 cup finely ground pork rinds (optional)

1/4 teaspoon garlic powder

1/2 jalapeno, finely chopped

2 tablespoons red onion, finely diced

2 tablespoons plain mayo

Avocado Cream Sauce:

1–2 tablespoons avocado oil

Salt and pepper, to taste

1 avocado

Juice of half lemon

1/4 cup sour cream

1–2 teaspoon water, to desired thickness

3 tablespoons cilantro

- Combine together all the salmon cake ingredients in a medium-sized bowl and shape into 5 to 6 small patties.
- Drizzle oil into a nonstick skillet and cook patties until brown and crispy on both sides, for 4 to 5 minutes over medium flame.
- Meanwhile, add all the avocado sauce ingredients to a food processor and blitz to combine until smooth.
- Serve delicious salmon cakes with sauce with an extra drizzle of mayo.

Herbed Almond And Parmesan Crusted Fish

Serves: 2-3 / Preparation time: 10 minutes / Cooking time: 40 minutes

2/3 cup crushed pork rinds

2 teaspoons Italian herb seasoning

1 lb. Alaska Pollock, frozen

2/3 cup Parmesan, freshly grated

3 oz. salted butter softened

Himalayan salt, to taste (optional)

- First, preheat your oven to a temperature of 350 °F (176 °C).
- Place fillets into a ceramic/glass baking dish.
- Mix together crushed pork rinds, butter, salt, Italian herb seasoning, and freshly grated parmesan in a medium-sized bowl using an electric mixer.
- Top fish fillets with this topping mixture.
- Bake until topping is golden brown, for 35 to 40 minutes.

Baked Lemon Butter Tilapia

Serves: 4 / Preparation time: 10 minutes / Cooking time: 10 minutes

Zest of 1 lemon

2 tablespoons parsley leaves, freshly chopped

1/4 cup unsalted butter, melted

Kosher salt and ground black pepper, to taste

3 cloves garlic, minced

4 (6-oz.) tilapia fillets

2 tablespoons lemon juice, freshly squeezed

- Preheat your oven to a temperature of 425°F (218°C).
- Coat a baking dish (9×13) with nonstick spray.
- Combine together 3 minced cloves of garlic, 1/4 cup butter, zest of one lemon, and 2 tablespoons lemon juice in a small-sized bowl. Keep it aside.
- Season the tilapia with pepper and salt and place it onto a baking dish.
- Drizzle over butter mixture.
- Bake in a preheated oven for about 10 to 12 minutes, until done.
- Garnish with parsley and enjoy!

BLT Lobster Roll Salad

Serves: 4 / Preparation time: 30 minutes / Cooking time: 0 minutes

For The Lobster Salad:

1 1/2 cups cauliflower florets, cooked until tender and chilled

1 teaspoon fresh tarragon leaves, chopped

2 cups lobster meat, cooked and chopped into bite-sized pieces

1/2 cup sugar-free mayonnaise

To Serve:

8 fresh romaine lettuce leaves

1/2 cup cooked bacon, chopped

1/2 cup tomatoes, chopped

- Combine together all the salad ingredients in a medium-sized bowl until creamy and well-combined.
- Lay leaves of lettuce onto a serving platter.
- Divide lobster mixture among 8 leaves and sprinkle each with chopped bacon and tomatoes.
- Serve as is or chilled!

Shrimp Cocktail with 3 Sauces

Serves: 8 / Preparation time: 5 minutes / Cooking time: 10 minutes

2 lbs. cooked shrimp, chilled

For The Keto Cocktail Sauce:

1 teaspoon lemon juice

1/4 teaspoon ground black pepper

1/2 cup reduced sugar ketchup

3 tablespoons prepared horseradish

1/2 teaspoon Worcestershire sauce

For The Pesto Mayonnaise:

1/4 cup basil pesto

1/2 cup mayonnaise

For The Spicy Sriracha Dipping Sauce:

2 tablespoons Sriracha

1 teaspoon lemon juice

1/2 cup mayonnaise

1 teaspoon granulated erythritol sweetener

- Place shrimp on a bed of ice until ready to serve.
- Serve with one or all sauces below.
- To Make The Pesto Mayonnaise: Mix together 1/4 cup basil pesto and 1/2 cup mayonnaise until well combined.
- Leftovers can be stored for up to 10 days in a refrigerator.
- To Make The Cocktail Sauce: Add all the cocktail sauce ingredients to a bowl and mix well.
- Leftovers can be stored for up to 10 days in a refrigerator.
- To Make the Sriracha Dipping Sauce: Add all the Sriracha dipping sauce ingredients to a bowl and mix well until combined.
- Leftovers can be stored for up to 10 days in a refrigerator.

Easy Shrimp Scampi

Serves: 6 / Preparation time: 20 minutes / Cooking time: 20 minutes

1/8 teaspoon ground black pepper

3 cups spaghetti squash, cooked

2 tablespoons butter

1 teaspoon lemon zest

2 tablespoons olive oil

2 tablespoons lemon juice

1 tablespoon garlic, minced

1/3 cup fresh parsley, chopped

1/2 cup dry white wine

2 lbs. extra-large shrimp, peeled and deveined

1/2 teaspoon kosher salt

1/3 teaspoon red pepper flakes (optional)

- Add 2 tablespoons of each butter and oil to a sauté pan and preheat over medium flame.
- Add in garlic and sauté until fragrant, for 2 to 3 minutes.
- Next, add in 1/4 teaspoon red pepper flakes, 1/2 cup dry white wine, 1/8 teaspoon ground black pepper, and 1/2 teaspoon kosher salt and continue cooking for another 2 minutes.
- Add shrimp and cook until opaque, for a few minutes.
- Turn the heat off and stir in 2 tablespoons lemon juice, 1 teaspoon lemon zest, and 1/3 cup chopped parsley.
- Serve delicious shrimp over warm, cooked spaghetti squash.
- Finish with a garnish of parmesan cheese, if desired.

Tuna Melts On Tomato Halves

Serves: 2 / Preparation time: 10 minutes / Cooking time: 9 minutes

1/2 cup cheddar cheese or any of your favorite cheese

Salt and pepper, to taste

2 large tomatoes, sliced into half and seeds removed

4 slices avocado

1 can flaked light tuna in water

4 pieces bacon, cooked

2 tablespoons mayo

2 pickles, sliced

2 to 4 tablespoons green onion, chopped

- Preheat your oven to a temperature of 400 degrees F (204.444°C).
- Scoop a can of tuna into a bowl and combine with chopped green onion and 2 tablespoons mayo.
- Place the tomatoes onto a baking sheet lined with parchment paper.
- Top each tomato half with half of the tuna mixture followed by slices of pickle and then cheese.
- Bake in a preheated oven until cheese is bubbly and melted, for 15 minutes.
- Once done, remove and serve immediately.

Smoky Tuna Pickle Boats

Serves: 12 pickle boats / Preparation time: 15 minutes / Cooking time: 0 minutes

6 large whole dill pickles, cut into half and seeds removed

2 six oz. cans (or pouches) albacore tuna

1/4 teaspoon ground black pepper

1 six oz. can (or pouch) smoked tuna

1/4 teaspoon garlic powder

1/3 cup sugar-free mayonnaise

1/2 teaspoon onion powder or 1 tablespoon dehydrated onion flakes

- Add all the ingredients to a medium-sized bowl except for pickles and combine well.
- Fill each pickle half with 3 tablespoons of tuna salad.
- Serve chilled!

Keto Fried Fish

Serves: 4 / Preparation time: 15 minutes / Cooking time: 15 minutes

Salt and pepper

Oil, for frying

1 lb. white fish cod, tilapia, or pollock

2 eggs, beaten

¾ cup almond flour

2 to 3 teaspoon creole seasoning

- Set your electric skillet to a temperature of 375°F (190°C). Alternatively, preheat oil in a heavy skillet over medium flame.
- Pour well-beaten eggs into a rectangular dish.
- Combine together creole seasoning and almond meal and add to a shallow dish.
- Pat the fish dry using clean paper towels, then season both of its sides with pepper and salt.
- Dip seasoned fish in egg, shaking off excess, if any.
- Then coat each fish piece with almond flour mixture on all sides.
- Cook fish in hot oil, each side, for 2 to 4 minutes. Time may vary depending upon the thickness of the fish.
- Once done, let it cool and enjoy!

Hazelnut Crusted Sea Bass

Serves: 2 to 3 / Preparation time: 15 minutes / Cooking time: 15 minutes

½ teaspoon garlic powder

1 tablespoon parsley, chopped

2 tablespoon butter

2 slices lemon

⅓ cup toasted hazelnuts, loose skins removed

Salt and pepper

½ teaspoon salt

2 (8 oz. each) sea bass fillets

½ teaspoon pepper

⅛ teaspoon cayenne

- First, preheat your oven to a temperature of 425° F (218°C).
- Add butter to a ceramic or glass baking dish (9x13) and melt it in the oven.
- In the meantime, add ½ teaspoon garlic powder, ⅓ cup toasted hazelnuts, pepper, salt, and ⅛ teaspoon cayenne to a food processor and blitz to combine until you have a few big pieces of hazelnut.
- Remove melted butter from the oven.
- Pat dry the sea bass with clean paper towels and lay in the pan, skin-side down.
- Spoon some of the butter, followed by a sprinkle of pepper and salt.
- Sprinkle with a mixture of hazelnut, pressing a bit to adhere.
- Squeeze slices of lemon over fillets and then lay on top.
- Bake in a preheated oven until fish flakes easily and is no longer opaque. It may take 15 to 17 minutes, so keep an eye on it.
- Take out from the oven and garnish with chopped parsley.
- After laying fillets in a serving platter, spoon the remaining butter from the dish onto them.
- Serve and enjoy!

Fantasy Fish Cakes

Serves: 3 / Preparation time: 4 minutes / Cooking time: 5 minutes

1 ½ tablespoon golden flax meal

2 tablespoon avocado/coconut/olive oil for frying

5 to 6 oz. can tuna fish or packet

¼ teaspoon onion powder

1 egg, beaten

¼ teaspoon garlic powder

1 tablespoon mayonnaise

⅛ teaspoon sea salt

2 tablespoon parmesan cheese

2 tablespoon almond meal or almond flour

The Aioli Sauce:

1 teaspoon lemon zest, grated

⅛ teaspoon black pepper

½ cup mayonnaise

⅛ teaspoon sea salt

3 cloves garlic, minced

1 teaspoon lemon juice

- Drain the tuna well, and then pat it dry with a clean paper towel.
- Add the entire list of ingredients to a medium-sized bowl except for olive oil. Mix well.
- Preheat oil in a pan and place a heaping spoonful of mixture into it, pressing and flattening with the back of the spatula or spoon a bit.
- Cook until browned and crusted, each side for 2 to 3 minutes.
- To prepare aioli sauce, add all its ingredients in a bowl and refrigerate until ready to use, covered.

Keto Fish Fingers With Chimichurri Mayo

Serves: 2 / Preparation time: 10 minutes / Cooking time: 15 minutes

1/2 teaspoon onion powder

1 1/2 tablespoons chimichurri

250 g white fish such as cod, cut into slices

1/4 cup paleo mayonnaise

1 large egg, lightly beaten

1/4 teaspoon paprika

1/3 cup almond flour

1/4 teaspoon garlic powder

1/2 teaspoon sea salt

Homemade Chimichurri Sauce:

1 small red chile pepper, seeds removed

1/4 teaspoon black pepper

1 large bunch of fresh parsley

1/2 teaspoon salt

1/4 cup fresh oregano

1/2 cup extra-virgin olive oil

4 cloves garlic, chopped

2 tablespoons apple cider vinegar or fresh lime juice

- Cut fish into "fingers" about an inch wide.
- Preheat your oven to a temperature of 410°F (210°C) for conventional, or 375°F (190 °C) for fan assisted.
- Crack an egg into a small bowl and beat well.
- Mix together all the dry ingredients in another shallow bowl.
- Line a baking tray with parchment paper and grease it.
- Now start dipping fish pieces, one by one, into an egg and then cat with the dry mixture on all sides, shaking off excess.
- Once done with all pieces, bake in a prepared tray for 7 to 8 minutes, then flip over the pieces and bake until golden brown for another 5 minutes.
- Meanwhile, prepare the sauce by mixing all the chimichurri ingredients in a blender.
- For chimichurri mayo, mix together chimichurri and mayo in a separate bowl.

- Serve delicious fish fingers with lemon wedges and mayo.

Almond and Parmesan Baked Fish

Serves: 4 / Preparation time: 15 minutes / Cooking time: 20 minutes

2 tablespoons parmesan cheese, finely grated

1 teaspoon Szeged fish rub (optional)

4 white fish filets, thawed if frozen

1/4 teaspoon pepper

1/4 cup melted butter

1/2 teaspoon garlic powder

1/3 cup almond flour

- First, preheat your oven to a temperature of 425°F (218°C).
- Grease your baking dish with nonstick spray.
- Add butter to a pan and melt over low flame.
- Combine together all the remaining ingredients except for fish in a large-sized bowl.
- Now coat each fish fillet with the almond-cheese mixture, until both sides are coated, pressing as much as you can.
- Bake in a preheated oven until the coating turns golden brown for about 20 minutes. The time may vary depending upon the fish thickness.
- Serve warm parmesan baked fish with double dill homemade tartar sauce.

Low-Carb Coconut Fish Curry With Spinach

Serves: 6 / Preparation time: 5 minutes / Cooking time: 20 minutes

1 ⅔ cups coconut cream

1.1 lbs. spinach, washed and sliced

2.2 lbs. firm white fish, cut into cubes

1 ⅔ cups water

2 to 4 tablespoons curry paste/powder of choice

- Preheat oil in a pan over medium-high heat and add in curry paste. Fry for just a few minutes over low.
- Add in 1 ⅔ cups water and 1 ⅔ cups coconut cream and bring it to a boil.
- Now add in fish pieces carefully and turn the heat down. Simmer for approximately 12 to 15 minutes.
- Next, add in prepared spinach and continue cooking until spinach has wilted, for 3 to 4 minutes.
- Serve warm!

Oven-Baked Fish

Serves: 2 / Preparation time: 10 minutes / Cooking time: 20 minutes

3 cloves garlic

1/4 teaspoon black pepper

12 oz. whiting

1/2 teaspoon pink Himalayan salt

2 tablespoons butter, chop into chunks

1/4 teaspoon onion powder

1 whole lime zest

1 whole lime, sliced

2 teaspoons ginger root, grated

- Place whiting in a flat layer at the bottom of your baking pan.
- Layer grated ginger and minced garlic onto the fish.
- Season the fish with lime zest, pepper, salt, and onion powder.
- Finally, top with lime slices and butter chunks.
- Cook for 20 minutes in the oven at 350°F (176°C).
- Serve immediately.

Low-Carb Cauliflower Sushi

Serves: 4 / Preparation time: 15 minutes / Cooking time: 0 minutes

1 tablespoon white vinegar

4 large nori sheets

1.1 lbs. raw cauliflower, including the stalk cut into chunks

Fish of choice

3.5 oz. cream cheese full fat

Vegetables of choice

1 spring onion, thinly sliced

Salt and pepper, to taste

- Add cauliflower chunks to a food processor and pulse until you have small pieces of cauliflower rice.
- Add in 1 tablespoon white vinegar, cream cheese, pepper, salt, and thinly sliced spring onion and continue processing until thoroughly mixed. Do not puree the mixture.
- Adjust the taste of cauliflower rice. You may like to add more salt or vinegar.
- Spread nori sheet with cheese cauliflower rice mixture, leaving 2 inches of the sheet bare.
- Place fish and your favorite veggies along the center, dampening the bare end and rolling up tightly.
- Repeat the same process with the remaining sheets.
- Once done with all, slice with a sharp wet knife and enjoy with coconut aminos/soy sauce, if desired.

Keto Fish Cakes With Roasted Red Pepper

Serves: 4 / Preparation time: 20 minutes / Cooking time: 10 minutes

For the Keto Fish Cakes:

2 tablespoons coconut flour

2 tablespoons olive oil for frying

1 lb. firm white fish, chopped into pieces of 1/2 inch in size

2 tablespoons fresh parsley, chopped

2 tablespoons parmesan cheese, grated

1 teaspoon creole seasoning

2 tablespoons sugar-free mayonnaise

1/2 teaspoon Worcestershire sauce or coconut aminos

1 egg

1 teaspoon Dijon mustard

For the Roasted Red Pepper Salsa:

1 tablespoon red onion, minced

1 teaspoon granulated erythritol sweetener

1/2 cup roasted red peppers, chopped

1 teaspoon lemon juice

1/4 cup fresh parsley, chopped

2 tablespoons extra virgin olive oil

1/2 teaspoon fresh garlic, minced

- Combine together chopped fish, 2 tablespoons mayonnaise, 2 tablespoons parmesan cheese, 2 tablespoons coconut flour, egg, 1/2 teaspoon Worcestershire sauce, 2 tablespoons fresh chopped parsley, 1 teaspoon creole seasoning, and 1 teaspoon Dijon mustard.
- Preheat oil in a nonstick pan. Once hot, shape mixture into 8 patties (each 2-in. wide)
- Fry patties until golden brown, each side for 2 minutes or until cooked through.
- Serve warm with roasted red pepper salsa.
- To make salsa, mix together all the salsa ingredients in a small bowl.
- Leftovers can be stored for up to a week in a refrigerator.

Zoodles With Sardines, Tomatoes & Capers

Serves: 2 / Preparation time: 10 minutes / Cooking time: 10 minutes

1/2 cup ripe tomatoes, chopped

1 tablespoon fresh parsley, chopped

4 oz. can of brisling sardines packed in olive oil

Salt and pepper, to taste

1 tablespoon extra-virgin olive oil

4 cups zucchini noodles

1 teaspoon garlic, chopped

1 tablespoon capers, drained

- Open the sardines and pour oil into a pan.
- Add in a tablespoon of olive oil.
- Cook garlic until fragrant for a minute or two.
- Next, add in tomatoes and caper and continue cooking for another minute.
- Now add sardines and cook for a minute.
- Stir in zucchini noodles for 2 to 4 minutes.
- Season the noodles with pepper and salt to taste.
- Finish with a garnish of parsley and top with parmesan cheese.
- Enjoy!

Vegetarian Recipes

Crispy Air Fryer Brussels sprouts

Serves: 4 / Preparation time: 5 minutes / Cooking time: 30 minutes

1 lb. Brussels sprouts, ends trimmed off

1 tablespoon olive oil

Sea salt, to taste

- First, preheat your air fryer to 350°F (176°C).
- Add Brussels to a bowl and toss with salt and olive oil, removing singular leaves, if any, and preserve for later use.
- Place Brussels sprouts in a mesh air fryer basket and let them cook for about 12 minutes.
- Then, shake the basket carefully and continue cooking until Brussels have cooked through, for about 10 to 12 minutes.
- In the last few minutes of cooking, toss with singular leaves and then remove to a serving platter.
- Serve and enjoy!

Roasted Air Fryer Cauliflower

Serves: 4 / Preparation time: 5 minutes / Cooking time: 22 minutes

3/4 lb. cauliflower, cut into florets

Sea salt, to taste

2 teaspoons olive oil

- Add cauliflower florets to a large-sized bowl and toss with oil until coated.
- Sprinkle with a generous pinch of salt and place in a mesh air fryer basket in a single layer.
- Cook for about 17 to 22 minutes at 400°F (204°C), or until tender and golden brown.
- Serve immediately!

Cauliflower Tabbouleh

Serves: 2 / Preparation time: 15 minutes / Cooking time: 6 minutes

1/2 cup parsley leaves, firmly packed

2 tablespoons olive oil

3 cups riced cauliflower

2 teaspoons fresh lemon juice

1 tomato on the vine, sliced into 4 chunks, scraping out watery insides

1 tablespoon fresh garlic, minced

1/2 cucumber, diced

1 green onion, sliced (green parts only)

1/2 teaspoon salt

1/4 cup mint leaves, firmly packed

- Add cauliflower to a microwave-safe bowl and heat for 3 minutes, covered. Stir well and continue heating for another 3 minutes. Then transfer to a clean kitchen towel and cool for a few minutes.
- Once cooled enough to handle, squeeze out as much water as possible out of the cauliflower. Then transfer to a bowl.
- Dice the thick tomato parts and add to a cauliflower bowl along with diced cucumber and salt. Stir well.
- Add mint and parsley to a food processor and process until you have tiny leaves. Stir into the cauliflower-cucumber mixture.
- Add in minced garlic and thinly sliced green parts of green onions and stir again.
- Add lemon juice to a small-sized bowl and whisk well with olive oil until you have a thickened mixture. Pour this dressing over cauliflower and toss everything once again.
- Cover the bowl, refrigerate for an hour & then serve!

Low Carb Mock Cauliflower Potato Salad

Serves: 8 / Preparation time: 10 minutes / Cooking time: 20 minutes

4 hard-boiled eggs, diced

1/4 cup red onion, diced

5 cups cauliflower, cut into florets

1/2 cup celery, thinly sliced

Sea salt

For The Dressing:

2 teaspoons sea salt

Pinch of pepper

9 tablespoons keto-friendly mayo

1/2 teaspoon paprika

5 teaspoons Dijon mustard

2 teaspoons dill paste

1 tablespoon apple cider vinegar

- Cook cauliflower in a pot of boiling salted water for about 9 to 10 minutes, or until fork-tender.
- Once cooked through, drain the cauliflower well and spread out onto a large paper towel sheet. Press out as much as possible using another paper towel and then transfer to a large-sized bowl.
- Add in diced eggs, red onion, and thinly sliced celery.
- Add all the dressing ingredients to another bowl and whisk well. Pour this dressing into a bowl with the cauliflower. Toss well until evenly coated.
- Refrigerate for 2 hours, covered.
- Season with pepper and salt to your preferences and serve chilled mock cauliflower potato salad.

Parmesan Roasted Ranch Cauliflower With Avocado

Serves: 4 / Preparation time: 10 minutes / Cooking time: 25 minutes

2 tablespoons ranch mix (recipe below)

1 large avocado, cubed

1 lb. cauliflower, cut into large florets

Pinch of sea salt

2 tablespoons olive oil

2 tablespoons parmesan cheese, finely grated

For Ranch Seasoning:

1 teaspoon garlic powder

1/3 teaspoon pepper

1 tablespoon dried parsley

3/4 teaspoon salt

1 teaspoon dried dill

1 teaspoon onion powder

- First, preheat your oven to 400°F (204°C).
- Add cauliflower to a large-sized bowl and toss with oil.
- Add all the ranch dressing ingredients to a separate bowl, whisk well and add tablespoons of this dressing into a bowl with the cauliflower. Toss well.
- Spread tossed cauliflower onto a large rimmed baking sheet evenly, leaving some space between each floret.
- First, cook for 15 minutes, stir well and continue cooking for another 10 to 12 minutes.
- Once cooked through, transfer cauliflower to another bowl and toss with finely grated parmesan, cubed avocado, and salt.
- Enjoy!

Instant Pot Green Beans

Serves: 4 / Preparation time: 5 minutes / Cooking time: 1 minute

1 cup water

1/2 teaspoon salt

1 lb. green beans, ends trimmed off

2 teaspoon garlic, minced

- Add trimmed beans to an Instant Pot machine along with the remaining ingredients and give everything a nice stir.
- Put on its lid and cook for 0 minutes on high pressure.
- Once done, let the steam release naturally.
- Open the lid and drain the green beans.
- Adjust salt to your preferences and enjoy it as is!

Air Fryer Asparagus

Serves: 2 / Preparation time: 5 minutes / Cooking time: 12 minutes

1 teaspoon garlic, minced

1 bunch of asparagus

Pinch of salt

1 teaspoon olive oil

- Remove the stalky ends of asparagus by breaking them.
- Toss with a teaspoon of minced garlic, a pinch of salt, and a teaspoon of olive oil.
- Put in an air fryer basket evenly and cook for about 12 minutes at 400 °F (204°C) or until fork tender.
- Wow, this delicious keto Mediterranean is so yummy!

Instant Pot Tomato Soup

Serves: 6 / Preparation time: 5 minutes / Cooking time: 25 minutes

2 cups chicken broth

1/2 cup whipping cream

1 1/2 lbs. Roma tomatoes

1/2-3/4 teaspoon salt, to taste

1 1/2 tablespoons olive oil

1 bay leaf

2 teaspoons garlic, minced

1 teaspoon dried basil

1/4 teaspoon salt

1 teaspoon dried oregano

1/8 teaspoon pepper

2 tablespoons tomato paste

Fresh basil, very thinly sliced (for serving)

- Add tomato cubes to a bowl and toss with ¼ teaspoon of salt, 2 teaspoons of minced garlic, 1 1/2 tablespoons olive oil, and 1/8 teaspoon pepper.
- Add tomatoes to an Instant Pot machine.
- Secure its lid to a sealing position and cook for 15 minutes on manual high.
- Once done, allow to release the pressure naturally. It may take some time. So, be patient.
- Transfer everything from pot to a blender and blitz to combine until smooth. Alternatively, you can use it with an immersion blender.
- Transfer back to an Instant pot along with remaining ingredients except for cream.
- Bring everything to a boil using the "Sauté" setting. Then turn the heat down to medium-low and continue simmering for about 7 minutes.
- Turn off your pot and stir in 1/2 cup whipping cream.
- Adjust the salt, if desired.
- Serve delicious tomato soup with basil, and enjoy!

Sautéed Broccolini

Serves: 4 / Preparation time: 5 minutes / Cooking time: 15 minutes

1 tablespoon olive oil

Salt, to taste

1 lb. broccolini, cut off the stalky ends and leaves removed

1/2 teaspoon garlic, diced

1/2 cup water

- Add broccolini to a high-sided, large skillet along with water and turn on the flame to medium.
- Cook for about 8 to 10 minutes, or until the stalks are fork tender and broccolini is bright green in color, covered, stirring occasionally.
- Remove cover and continue cooking for a minute or two until almost most of the water has dried.
- Push broccolini to one side of the skillet and add oil to the center along with garlic. Cook until broccolini has charred and browned a bit, stirring.
- Adjust the salt, if needed, and serve warm!

Keto Cabbage Rolls

Serves: 6 / Preparation time: 30 minutes / Cooking time: 1 hour

1 lb. 90% lean ground beef	2 cups cauliflower rice
2 cups marinara sauce, divided	1 teaspoon salt
1 large head of green cabbage	1/4 cup onions, diced
1 egg, whisked	2 teaspoons Italian seasoning
1/2 tablespoon olive oil	1 teaspoon fresh garlic
Pinch of ground nutmeg	1/4 cup fresh parsley, minced

- First, preheat your oven to 350 °F (176°C).
- Pour 3/4 cup of tomato sauce into a pan of 9×13 inches.
- Cook head of cabbage in a very large pot of boiling water for about 4 to 6 minutes, until the leaves are bright green. Make sure to completely submerge the cabbage head in the water. Once done, drain well and let it cool.
- In the meantime, preheat oil in a pan and add cauliflower, garlic, and onion. Cook for 5 minutes and then add in leftover ingredients and a half cup of tomato sauce. Stir well.
- Peel off the 12 leaves from the cabbage and place them onto a flat surface. Remove the hard part of leaves by cutting v shape on the bottom.
- Take 1/12 of the mixture and shape it into a log. Place this log in mid of each cabbage, rolling up like a burrito, tucking the sides in, and rolling it up from down to up.
- Place roll in the bottom of prepared pan in a way that seam-side remains down.
- Do the same with leftover leaves.
- Pour remaining tomato sauce over rolls and bake until beef is done. It will take an hour at least.
- Cover it tightly while baking.
- Once done, let them cool and serve!

Mediterranean Cucumber Salad

Serves: 4 / Preparation time: 5 minutes / Cooking time: 0 minutes

1/4 red onion, sliced

1/4 teaspoon salt

2 tablespoons olive oil

2 teaspoons dukkah seasoning

2 tablespoons fresh lemon juice

1 tablespoon fresh mint, minced

1 cucumber, thinly sliced

- Add lemon juice to a medium-sized bowl and whisk well. Meanwhile, stream in oil and continue whisking until thickened.
- Add in remaining ingredients and toss everything well.
- Chill for an hour, covered.
- Keto Mediterranean cucumber salad is ready to serve!

Paleo Low Carb Keto Beef And Broccoli

Serves: 2 / Preparation time: 10 minutes / Cooking time: 15 minutes

2 1/2 cups broccoli, large florets

Cooked cauliflower rice

1/4 cup coconut aminos, divided

Sesame seeds, for garnish

1 teaspoon fresh ginger, minced and divided

Green onion, for garnish

1 teaspoon fresh garlic, minced and divided

Salt, to taste

8 oz. flank steak, sliced

1/2 teaspoon sesame oil

1 1/2 tablespoons avocado oil, divided

1/4 cup reduced-sodium beef broth

- Whisk together with 1/2 teaspoon of ginger, 1/2teaspoon of garlic, and a tablespoon of coconut aminos.
- Add beef to this bowl, stir and refrigerate for an hour, covered.
- Preheat a tablespoon of oil in a pan and add broccoli. Cook for 3 to 4 minutes, until it just begins to soften, stirring continuously.
- Add in remaining ginger and garlic and continue cooking for another one minute.
- Turn down the heat to low and cook for a further 4 to 5 minutes, until broccoli I tender, stirring often.
- Once done, remove broccoli to a platter and raise the heat. Add remaining oil to the pan along with marinated beef and cook for 2 to 3 minutes, until golden brown.
- Transfer broccoli back to the pan and stir well.
- Whisk together 1/4 cup reduced-sodium beef broth, 1/2 teaspoon sesame oil, and rest f coconut aminos in a small-sized bowl and pour into a pan. Continue cooking for a minute or two until it starts to thicken, stirring continuously.
- Adjust the salt, if desired.

- Serve over cauliflower rice and finish with a garnishing of sesame seeds and green onion.

French Fries

Serves: 4 / Preparation time: 10 minutes / Cooking time: 25 minutes

1 1/4 lb. rutabaga, peeled and sliced into 1/4 inch thick strips

Salt, to taste

1 1/2 tablespoons olive

- First, preheat your oven to 425°F (218°C).
- Place a cooling rack (oven safe) on a large baking sheet.
- Add rutabaga strips to a large bowl and drizzle with oil. Toss well, and then sprinkle with a generous pinch of salt.
- Place rutabaga onto a cooling rack, leaving a room between each fry. Do this in two baking sheets, if desired.
- Bake in a preheated oven for 12 minutes, then flip over and continue cooking for another 10 to 15 minutes until the fries turn golden brown.
- Wow! Too yum!

Sandwich Wraps – Sun-dried Tomato & Basil

Serves: 4 / Preparation time: 5 minutes / Cooking time: 10 minutes

- 1/2 teaspoon psyllium husk powder
- Avocado oil spray for the pan
- 6 large eggs
- 1/4 teaspoon garlic powder
- 1 teaspoon white vinegar
- 1/4 teaspoon kosher salt
- 1/4 cup sun-dried tomatoes (dry, not in oil)
- 1/2 teaspoon dried basil
- 2 tablespoons coconut flour

- Add all the ingredients to a blender except for oil spray and blitz to combine until smooth.
- Preheat a nonstick pan and spray with avocado oil spray lightly.
- Pour about ¼ of the batter into the pan and spread evenly using a rubber spatula.
- Cook until just firm for a minute, then flip over and cook another side for 30 seconds.
- Once done, remove to a platter and repeat the same until you have 4 wraps.
- Keto sandwich wraps can be stored in an air-tight container for up to a week in the refrigerator or up to 6 months in the freezer.
- Bring to a room temperature just before serving.

Kale Salad With Goat Cheese And Pomegranate

Serves: 8 / Preparation time: 15 minutes / Cooking time: 1 minute

½ teaspoon salt

8 oz. goat cheese or feta cheese

12 oz. kale, washed, dried, stem/ribs trimmed off, and leaves chopped into bite-sized pieces

½ pomegranate, peeled and seeds separated

2 tablespoons olive oil

½ cup (2⅓ oz.) pumpkin seeds

For Vinaigrette:

1 tablespoon Dijon mustard

Sea salt and ground black pepper

½ cup olive oil

3 tablespoons orange juice

2 tablespoons balsamic vinegar

- Add kale leaves to a large-sized bowl. Put oil and season with a pinch of salt. Massage kale leaves until they darken in color, using your hands.
- Add pumpkin seeds to a frying pan and dry roast for 30 seconds. Keep them aside.
- Add all the vinaigrette ingredients to a bowl and whisk well. Pour this dressing over kale and toss well.
- Add almost all of the pomegranate seeds and pumpkin seeds, reserving some for garnish. Toss everything together.
- Crumble goat cheese over the salad and garnish with preserved pumpkin and pomegranate seeds.
- Season with salt and pepper to your preferences.

Keto Goat Cheese And Mushroom Frittata

Serves: 2 / Preparation time: 5 minutes / Cooking time: 30 minutes

For Frittata:

2 oz. butter

Salt and pepper

5 oz. mushrooms, cut into wedges

4 oz. goat cheese, grated or crumbled

3 oz. (2¾ cups) fresh spinach

6 eggs

2 oz. (9 tablespoons) scallions, chopped

For Serving:

5 oz. (2½ cups) leafy greens

Salt and pepper, to taste

2 tablespoons olive oil

- First, preheat your oven to 350°F (176°C).
- Crack eggs into a medium-sized bowl and whisk well.
- Add in pepper, salt, and grated/crumbled goat cheese.
- Add butter to an oven-proof skillet and let it melt. Add in mushroom wedges and chopped scallions and cook until golden brown for 10 to 15 minutes.
- Add in spinach and continue sautéing for a minute or two.
- Season with pepper and salt.
- Pour egg-cream mixture into a skillet and place it inside the oven. Bake until golden brown, for about 20 minutes, positioned in the middle rack.
- Serve keto goat cheese and mushroom frittata with leafy greens and olive oil.

Chopped Mediterranean Salad

Serves: 6 / Preparation time: 10 minutes / Cooking time: 0 minutes

For Mediterranean Salad:

1 cup artichoke hearts, chopped

1/2 cup feta cheese, crumbled

2 cup grape tomatoes, halved

1/3 cup red onion, sliced thinly

2 cup cucumber, chopped

For Sun-Dried Tomato Vinaigrette Dressing:

4 teaspoons apple cider vinegar

1/8 teaspoon black pepper

6 tablespoons olive oil

1/4 teaspoon sea salt

2 tablespoons sun-dried tomatoes (packed in oil)

1 clove garlic

- Puree all the sun-dried tomato vinaigrette dressing ingredients in a blender until smooth and emulsified. If it's too much thick, you can add a little water or oil and puree again.
- Add all the salad ingredients to a large-sized bowl and toss with dressing.

Green Beans and Avocado

Serves: 4 / Preparation time: 10 minutes / Cooking time: 5 minutes

¼ teaspoon ground black pepper

Fresh cilantro (optional)

3 tablespoons olive oil

5 (2 2/3 oz.) scallions, finely chopped

2/3 lb. fresh green beans, trimmed

2 (14 oz.) ripe avocados, peeled and pitted

½ teaspoon sea salt

- Preheat oil in a pan and sauté beans until tender and browned, for 3 to 4 minutes.
- Turn the heat down, add in spices, and transfer to a bowl.
- Add mashed avocado to a bowl along with onions and mix well.
- Garnish with cilantro just before serving.

Feta Cheese Stuffed Bell Peppers

Serves: 2 / Preparation time: 10 minutes / Cooking time: 20 minutes

10 green olives, pitted and chopped

1 teaspoon hot sauce

2 (10 oz.) green bell peppers, cut in half lengthwise and seeds removed

½ tablespoons dried mint

11 oz. (2 cups) feta cheese

2 eggs

For Serving:

1 oz. (½ cup) leafy greens

1 pinch sea salt

2 tablespoons olive oil

- Preheat the oven to 400° F (204°C).
- Add all the ingredients to a bowl except for green bell peppers and mix well.
- Stuff peppers with cheese filling mixture and place them in a baking tray/baking dish.
- Bake until golden brown on top, for about 20 minutes.
- Serve as is or with a salad!

Mediterranean Low Carb Broccoli Salad

Serves: 8 / Preparation time: 25 minutes / Cooking time: 0 minutes

For The Salad:

1/2 cup sun-dried tomatoes in olive oil, chopped

1/2 cup artichoke hearts marinated in olive oil, sliced

1/2 cup pitted kalamata olives, halved

1/4 cup roasted salted sunflower seeds

5 cups broccoli, cut into small florets

1/3 cup red onion, diced

For The Dressing:

1 1/2 teaspoon fresh garlic, minced

2 tablespoons oil from the jar of sun-dried tomatoes

2 cups plain, non-fat Greek yogurt

Pepper

4 1/2 teaspoon monkfruit

Zest and juice of 1 large lemon

1 teaspoon sea salt

1 1/2 teaspoons dried ground thyme

1 3/4 teaspoons dried oregano

1 1/2 teaspoons dried ground basil

- Add all the salad ingredients to a bowl and mix well.
- Take another bowl and whisk together all the dressing ingredients.
- Pour dressing over salad and toss well until coated.
- Refrigerate at least for 2 hours, covered.
- Serve chilled!

Easy Vegan Cauliflower Fried Rice

Serves: 4 / Preparation time: 15 minutes / Cooking time: 15 minutes

2 carrots, diced

Sesame seeds, for garnish

1 lb. firm tofu, pressed and drained

3 tablespoons soy sauce

1 medium-sized head of cauliflower, cut into florets, discarding the tough inner core

3 tablespoons cashews

2 tablespoons sesame oil, divided

1/4 cup green onions, thinly sliced

1 tablespoon ginger, minced

1/2 cup peas, thawed if frozen

3 cloves garlic, minced

- Press and drain the tofu. Do this by wrapping it in clean paper towels and pressing with a heavy object.
- Add tofu to a large-sized bowl and crumble lightly. Keep it aside.
- Add cauliflower florets to a food processor and process until you have rice-sized pieces. Keep kit aside.
- Preheat sesame oil in a large-sized wok and add in garlic and ginger. Cook until golden brown, for30 seconds, stirring frequently.
- Add in crumbled tofu and continue stir-frying until tofu becomes golden in color, stirring often.
- Once done, remove tofu from work and ass in remaining sesame oil. Add in diced carrot and sauté for 2 minutes, until tender.
- Add cauliflower rice to the wok along with peas and mix well.
- Cook for 5 to 8 minutes, until cauliflower is tender, stirring often.
- Stir in 3 tablespoons cashews, 1/4 cup thinly sliced green onions, 3 tablespoons soy sauce, and cooked tofu.
- Finish with a garnish of sesame seeds and serve immediately.

Mediterranean Collard Green Wraps

Serves: 4 / Preparation time: 15 minutes / Cooking time: 0 minutes

1/2 large bell pepper, cut into thin strips

1 medium avocado, sliced

4 large collard leaves, washed, dried, and shaved off the thick part of the stems

1/4 cup red onion, sliced into thin half moons

1/2 cup cauliflower hummus

1 medium Roma tomato, diced

3 oz. cucumber, cut into thin and short strips

- Lay out the collar leaves and top each with 2 tablespoons of cauliflower hummus, leaving an inch of border empty. Spread the hummus evenly and top with cucumber strips, bell pepper strips, red onion half-moons, diced tomato, and sliced avocado.
- Place all these veggies perpendicular to the leaf's length.
- Start wrapping the collard green wraps with the wide side. Ends should be folded first before rolling up like a burrito.
- Do the same with remaining collard wraps and serve immediately.

Spinach Quiche with Crust

Serves: 10 / Preparation time: 15 minutes / Cooking time: 50 minutes

For Crust:

2 oz. butter melted

1 pinch pepper ground

2 cups almond flour

1 pinch salt

1 egg

For Filling:

4 large eggs

4 oz. jarlsberg cheese, shredded

1 tablespoon olive oil

½ teaspoon pepper ground

2 cloves garlic, crushed

1 teaspoon salt

10 oz. spinach

1 cup heavy crea

- Preheat the oven to 340°F (171°C).
- Combine together all the crust ingredients in a bowl.
- Press into the base of your quiche dish and up the sides.
- Bake in a preheated oven for 12 to 15 minutes.
- To prepare the filling, add oil to a pan and heat over medium-high flame.
- Sauté spinach and garlic with a pinch of salt until cooked through. It may take 5 to 8 minutes.
- Add cooked spinach to a colander to drain excess liquid.
- Add spinach to a baked crust and spread evenly.
- Sprinkle top with cheese.
- Mix together 1 cup heavy cream, 4 large eggs, 1 teaspoon salt, and ½ teaspoon pepper ground in a medium-sized bowl and pour over the spinach.

- Bake in a preheated oven until the center doesn't jiggle when removed. It will take approximately 25-35 minutes.
- Once done, remove from oven and cut into 10 slices.
- It's ready!

Garlic Butter Mushrooms

Serves: 2 / Preparation time: 10 minutes / Cooking time: 20 minutes

¼ teaspoon pepper ground

2 tablespoons parsley, chopped

1 tablespoon olive oil

3 tablespoons butter

4 cloves garlic, finely chopped

1 lb. button mushrooms

1 teaspoon sea salt flakes

- Preheat oil in a large nonstick pan. Once hot, add in garlic along with pepper and salt and cook until fragrant.
- Next, add mushrooms and stir until coated with the mixture.
- Now start adding butter, 1 tablespoon at a time, allow mushrooms to coat with it after each addition.
- Once mushrooms begin to release liquid, turn the heat down and cook until their color turns a deep brown, occasionally stirring, for 10 to 15 minutes.
- Turn off the flame, stir in parsley and serve immediately!

Garlic Green Beans with Slivered Almonds

Serves: 4 / Preparation time: 5 minutes / Cooking time: 10 minutes

2 tablespoons butter

¼ cup slivered almonds

1 lb. green beans

2 teaspoons salt flakes

2 tablespoons olive oil

2 cloves garlic, thinly sliced

- Boil the beans until tender for about 5 minutes and then drain well.
- Add oil to a nonstick pan along with butter, salt, and garlic—Cook for 4 minutes.
- Next, add in almonds and continue sautéing until almonds turn brown.
- Stir in green beans for 3 minutes and serve warm!
- Simple as that!

Roasted Beetroot & Goat's Cheese Salad

Serves: 6 sides or 3 mains / Preparation time: 15 minutes / Cooking time: 45 minutes

Salad:

1 cup walnuts, chopped

1 (50 g/ 1.8 oz.) pack arugula (rocket)

Pinch of salt

200 g soft goat's cheese

3 whole fresh beetroots

Balsamic Vinaigrette:

1 teaspoon confectioner's Swerve or Erythritol

Pinch of salt

4 tablespoons balsamic vinegar

1 teaspoon Dijon mustard

2 tablespoons extra virgin olive oil

- First, preheat the oven to 355 ° F (179°C).
- Wrap washed beetroot in aluminum foil and place it in a baking tray—Bake in a preheated oven for 45 minutes.
- Meanwhile, add all the dressing ingredients to a jar and shake until combined.
- Once the beetroot is done, remove it from the oven and let it cool.
- Peel off the skin of beetroots using your fingers. Then cut into wedges and keep them aside.
- Add rocket to a serving bowl and toss with some of the dressing.
- Top with beetroot wedges followed by a sprinkle of walnuts, pieces of goat's cheese, and dressing in last.
- Chill in the refrigerator, covered.
- Enjoy chilled roasted beetroot & goat's cheese salad!

Low-Carb Heirloom Tomato Salad Bowl

Serves: 6 / Preparation time: 20 minutes / Cooking time: 0 minutes

2 tablespoons capers

Black pepper, to taste

1.35 kg heirloom tomatoes, sliced

Generous pinch flaky sea salt

1/2 cup torn fresh herbs such as basil, dill, parsley, mint)

1 tablespoon white balsamic vinegar

1/2 cup feta cheese, crumbled

3 tablespoons extra virgin olive oil

- Chop the herbs after washing them.
- Arrange sliced tomatoes in a serving bowl or platter.
- Top with cheese, capers, and chopped herbs.
- Drizzle everything with vinegar and olive oil.
- Season the salad with pepper and salt to your preferences.
- Serve fresh!

Seafood Salad With Avocado

Serves: 6 / Preparation time: 20 minutes / Cooking time: 0 minutes

For Salad Dressing:

1 garlic clove, minced

¼ teaspoon white pepper

2 tablespoons lime juice

¼ cup red onions, finely minced

½ cup mayonnaise

1 teaspoon salt

1/3 cup sour cream

For Seafood Salad:

2½ oz. tomatoes, chopped (optional)

2 tablespoons fresh basil, roughly sliced

1 lb. shrimp, cooked and chopped

1 avocado, chopped

1 lb. boneless salmon fillets, cooked and cut into bite-sized pieces

1½ oz. cucumber, deseeded and finely chopped

- Combine together all the dressing ingredients in a medium-sized bowl and set aside.
- Add all the salad ingredients to another bowl except for basil and combine well.
- Pour dressing over veggies and seafood and toss well.
- Garnish with basil and chill for half an hour before serving.

Chicken BLT Salad

Serves: 4 / Preparation time: 5 minutes / Cooking time: 30 minutes

For Garlic Mayonnaise:

½ tablespoon garlic powder

¾ cup mayonnaise

For BLT:

1 lb. boneless chicken thighs

4 oz. cherry tomatoes, in halves

8 oz. bacon

10 oz. Romaine lettuce, rinsed and chopped

1 oz. butter (optional)

Salt and pepper, to taste

- Combine together ½ tablespoon garlic powder and ¾ cup mayonnaise in a small-sized bowl and set aside.
- Fry slices of bacon in butter until crispy. Then remove to a plate, leaving the grease behind.
- Season the chicken thighs with pepper and salt to taste.
- Slice each chicken thigh into thirds.
- Fry chicken thigh pieces in the same pan until cooked through.
- Spread lettuce onto a serving platter and top with cooked bacon slices, chicken, and tomatoes.
- Finish with a drizzle of garlic mayo sauce and enjoy!

Warm Kale Salad

Serves: 4 / Preparation time: 10 minutes / Cooking time: 10 minutes

1 garlic clove, minced or finely chopped

4 oz. blue cheese or feta cheese

¾ cup heavy whipping cream

8 oz. kale, rinsed and cut into bite-sized pieces (thick stems removed)

2 tablespoons mayonnaise or vegan mayonnaise

1 oz. butter

1 teaspoon Dijon mustard

Salt and pepper, to taste

2 tablespoons olive oil

- Combine together 2 tablespoons mayonnaise or vegan mayonnaise, 1 teaspoon Dijon mustard, 2 tablespoons olive oil, ¾ cup heavy whipping cream, and minced garlic. Season the bowl with pepper and salt to taste.
- Preheat butter in a large frying pan and cook kale until it turns a nice color. Season the kale with pepper and salt to taste.
- Add kale to a bowl and pour overdressing. Toss well and serve with crumbled blue cheese or any other of your favorite.

Keto Cauliflower 'Potato' Salad

Serves: 6 / Preparation time: 10 minutes / Cooking time: 25 minutes

For Cauliflower Salad:

5 oz. bacon

2 tablespoons fresh chives, diced

1½ lbs. cauliflower, chopped into bite-sized chunks

½ red onion, diced

Salt and ground black pepper, to taste

3 celery stalks, chopped

½ cup water

For Dressing:

¾ tablespoon cider vinegar

1 pinch ground black pepper

1½ cups mayonnaise

1 pinch salt

¾ tablespoon Dijon mustard

- Preheat a grill over low heat.
- Divide cauliflower pieces among two aluminum foil sheets evenly. Season the pieces with pepper and salt to taste.
- Lift the edges of the foil slightly so that it covers the pieces.
- Pour ¼ cup of water onto each package and wrap with another piece of aluminum foil so that water will not escape.
- Place cauliflower package onto a grill on the side and grill for 15 to 20 minutes.
- Place bacon slices in a grill pan having high ridges and grill until crisp for 10 to 15 minutes, flipping them once in between.
- Once cooked through, remove bacon slices from the grill and chop them into small pieces.
- Remove cauliflower package and unwrap carefully. Once cooled enough, add to a big bowl.
- Add in diced chives, onion, chopped bacon, and celery, reserving some of the pieces for garnishing.

- To prepare the dressing, add all the dressing ingredients to a bowl and mix well.
- Pour this dressing over the salad and toss until coated.
- Garnish with diced chives and chopped bacon.

Salad Sandwiches

Serves: 1 / Preparation time: 5 minutes / Cooking time: 0 minutes

4 tablespoons cheese

4 cherry tomatoes, sliced

2 oz. Romaine lettuce

½ avocado, sliced

- Lay lettuce leaves onto a serving platter.
- Spread leaves with mayonnaise or butter.
- Layer with cheese followed by sliced avocado and tomato over the top.
- It's so simple!

Wedge Salad

Serves: 4 / Preparation time: 7 minutes / Cooking time: 8 minutes

For Blue Cheese Dressing:

1 tablespoon lemon juice

2 oz. blue cheese, crumbled

1/3 cup mayonnaise

¼ teaspoon salt

¼ cup sour cream

¼ teaspoon garlic powder

2 tablespoons heavy whipping cream

For Salad:

½ head iceberg lettuce

1 tomato, chopped

8 oz. bacon, chopped

- Add all the dressing ingredients to a bowl except for cheese and mix well. Once well blended, stir in crumbles of blue cheese. You can thin the dressing with a small amount of water.
- Chill the dressing until ready to use.
- Add bacon to a frying pan and fry until crisp over medium heat.
- Rinse iceberg lettuce in cold water, drain well and pat it dry with a clean towel.
- Cut cauliflower head into half and cut one half into 4 pieces.
- Do not touch the remaining half head.
- Place each cauliflower wedge onto a serving platter and top with chopped tomato, bacon, cheese crumbles, and egg. All should be of equal amounts.
- Pour over the dressing and serve right away!

French Onion Dip

Serves: 6 / Preparation time: 5 minutes / Cooking time: 20 minutes

4 oz. sour cream	½ teaspoon cayenne pepper
½ teaspoon black pepper	2 cloves garlic, minced
2 medium onions, finely chopped	½ teaspoon onion powder
½ teaspoon salt	4 oz. cream cheese softened
2 tablespoons butter	2 oz. mayonnaise

- Add butter to a pan and preheat over medium flame.
- Add in 2 minced cloves of garlic, ½ teaspoon onion powder, ½ teaspoon cayenne pepper, ½ teaspoon salt, ½ teaspoon black pepper, and finely chopped onions.
- Cook everything for 5 minutes, stirring often.
- Then reduce the flame and continue cooking until onions turn golden, for another 15 to 20 minutes. Once done, remove and let it cool.
- Combine together sour cream, cream cheese, and mayonnaise in a medium-sized bowl and stir in cooked onions.
- Refrigerate for half an hour before serving.
- French onion dip is too yummy to eat!

Radish Potato Salad

Serves: 6 / Preparation time: 10 minutes / Cooking time: 10 minutes

½ cup celery, chopped

¼ cup red onion, finely chopped

4 cups radishes, trimmed and cut in half

3 medium hard-boiled eggs, peeled and cut

For Dressing:

3 tablespoons dill, chopped

½ teaspoon black pepper

⅓ cup mayonnaise

½ teaspoon salt

½ teaspoon garlic powder

½ teaspoon celery salt

1 tablespoon lemon juice

- Add radishes to a saucepan along with water and bring to a boil. Then simmer for approximately 10 minutes.
- Once done, drain well and keep aside.
- Add all the dressing ingredients to a bowl and mix well.
- Add drained radishes to a large-sized bowl and add in the remaining ingredients.
- Pour over the dressing and toss well until combined.
- Serve delicious radish potato chilled!

Spinach Ricotta Ravioli

Serves: 6 / Preparation time: 5 minutes / Cooking time: 10 minutes

6 slices provolone cheese

For Filling:

1 tablespoon parmesan vegetarian

¼ teaspoon nutmeg

¼ cup ricotta cheese

1 teaspoon black pepper

½ cup spinach, cooked

1 teaspoon salt

To Serve:

½ cup marinara sauce

- Preheat the oven to 350°F (176°C).
- Line a baking sheet with parchment paper and lay provolone cheese slices onto it.
- Bake in a preheated oven until edges are golden brown, for about 5 minutes.
- Combine together ½ cup cooked spinach, ¼ cup ricotta cheese, and 1 tablespoon parmesan in a medium-sized bowl and season it with 1 teaspoon salt, ¼ teaspoon nutmeg, and 1 teaspoon black pepper.
- Once cheese slices are done, remove them from the oven and spoon over a large tablespoon of spinach-cheese mixture on one side of each slice of provolone.
- Fold the slice over spinach-cheese filling, pressing down the edges to join.
- Bake for another 3 minutes and then serve with marinara or any of your favorite sauces.

Celery Soup

Serves: 8 / Preparation time: 10 minutes / Cooking time: 30 minutes

3 cups vegetable stock

½ teaspoon black pepper

2 medium shallots, chopped

½ teaspoon salt

3 cloves garlic, peeled and sliced

½ teaspoon celery pepper

2 tablespoons coconut oil

½ teaspoon celery salt

4 cups celery, chopped

2 tablespoons nutritional yeast

1 cup cauliflower florets

¼ teaspoon turmeric

- Preheat coconut oil in a large saucepan over medium flame.
- Sauté the shallots and garlic together until softened, for 5 minutes.
- Stir in cauliflower florets until coated with oil.
- Next, stir in chopped celery and cook for 5 minutes, covered.
- Add in seasoning, turmeric, yeast, and stock.
- Bring everything to a boil and then simmer at low for 15 to 20 minutes, or until veggies are tender.
- Once done, turn off the flame and let it cool a bit.
- Puree the soup using an immersion blender and garnish with celery leaves.

Spicy Green Omelet

Serves: 1 / Preparation time: 5 minutes / Cooking time: 10 minutes

Salt and pepper, for seasoning

2 large eggs

1 green chili pepper, seeded and finely sliced

1 cup watercress or baby spinach, roughly chopped

2 tablespoons fresh cilantro, finely chopped

1 oz. cheddar cheese, shredded

2 tablespoons heavy whipping cream

1 tablespoon butter

- Crack eggs into a medium-sized bowl and stir in 2 tablespoons heavy whipping cream, 2 tablespoons chopped cilantro, and finely sliced green chili until well combined.
- Season the eggs with a generous pinch of pepper and salt. Keep it aside.
- Add butter to a nonstick pan let it melt over medium-high heat. Pour in egg mixture and cook until bottom is set.
- Then flip over and cook another side until done.
- Top with cheese and watercress and cook for a few more minutes at low, covered.
- Slide omelet onto a serving platter and serve warm!

Low Crab Cauliflower Mac Cheese Recipe

Serves: 4 / Preparation time: 5 minutes / Cooking time: 20 minutes

Black pepper

1/4 cup unsweetened almond milk

1 head cauliflower, cut into small florets

1/4 cup heavy cream

1+2 tablespoons butter

1 cup cheddar cheese, shredded

Sea salt

- Preheat your oven to a temperature of 450° F (232°C).
- Take a baking sheet and line it with parchment paper or foil.
- Toss cauliflower florets with 2 tablespoons of melted butter and season them with pepper and salt to taste.
- Arrange florets onto a prepared baking sheet and roast in a preheated oven until crisp-tender, for 10 to 15 minutes.
- Microwave remaining butter, heavy cream, cheddar cheese, and milk in a medium-sized bowl, stirring frequently.
- Once smooth, toss cauliflower in this cheesy sauce.
- Serve and enjoy!

Latkes

Serves: 3 / Preparation time: 15 minutes / Cooking time: 10 minutes

2 large eggs

3 tablespoons sour cream

1/2 head cauliflower, grated

3 tablespoons salted butter

1/2 cup scallions, thinly sliced

1/2 teaspoon pepper

1 tablespoon golden flax meal

1 1/2 teaspoons salt

- Add grated cauliflower to a bowl and toss with a teaspoon of salt. Leave for 20 minutes.
- Spoon cauliflower into a clean towel and squeeze out the liquid as much as possible.
- Transfer squeezed cauliflower to a bowl along with remaining ingredients except for sour cream and butter. Combine well.
- Preheat butter in a nonstick pan and add spoonfuls of cauliflower mix, smoothing into small pancakes.
- Fry for 5 to 6 minutes, each side for 2 to 3 minutes.
- Once golden brown, remove and serve with sour cream!

Desserts

Peanut Butter & Chocolate Pie

Serves: 12 / Preparation time: 30 minutes / Cooking time: 10 minutes

For The Chocolate Crust:

2 cups superfine, blanched almond flour

7 tablespoons butter, melted

3 tablespoons cocoa powder

1/3 cup granulated erythritol sweetener

For The Filling:

1 3/4 cups heavy whipping cream

1/2 cup powdered erythritol

8 oz. mascarpone cheese, room temperature

1/4 teaspoon xanthan gum

2/3 cup sugar-free creamy peanut butter, room temperature

1/2 teaspoon vanilla

For The Topping:

1 tablespoon heavy whipping cream

1/4 cup salted peanuts, chopped

4 squares Lindt 90% chocolate

1 tablespoon powdered erythritol

2 tablespoons sugar-free peanut butter

- For the chocolate crust: First, preheat your oven to a temperature of 350° F (176.667°C).
- Combine together all the chocolate crust ingredients in a medium-sized bowl and transfer to a pie plate (9-inch), pressing the crust into the bottom of the pie plate and up the sides.
- Bake for about 10 minutes. Once done, let it cool.
- For the filling: Stir together 2/3 cup creamy peanut butter and 8 oz. mascarpone cheese, until creamy.
- Combine together remaining filling ingredients in a separate bowl until stiff peaks form.
- Start folding the peanut butter mixture into vanilla cream mixture.
- Spread cooled crust with this filling and smooth the top using a spatula. Freeze for half an hour.
- For the topping: Combine together 1 tablespoon heavy whipping cream, 2 tablespoons peanut butter, and 1 tablespoon powdered erythritol in a bowl. Spoon this mixture into a plastic baggie, snipping the tip off one corner.

- Squeeze lines of this mixture onto the top of your pie.
- Add chocolate to a microwave-safe bowl and heat until melted.
- Transfer melted into a plastic baggie, snipping the tip off one corner.
- Drizzle chocolate over the top of the pie, followed by a sprinkle of chopped peanuts.
- Serve as is or freeze for 2 hours at least.

Low Carb Peanut Butter & Chocolate Truffles

Serves: 18 / Preparation time: 30 minutes / Cooking time: 0 minutes

For The Truffles:

1 teaspoon vanilla extract

1/3 cup granulated sugar substitute

1 cup natural chunky peanut butter, room temperature (sugar-free)

3 tablespoons heavy whipping cream

1/3 cup zero carb vanilla protein powder

2 tablespoons unsalted butter, softened

For The Coating:

2 squares 85% (or more) cocoa dark chocolate

OR

2 tablespoons unsweetened cocoa powder

- Add all the ingredients to a food processor and whip until well incorporated.
- Roll into 18 truffles (one inch each).
- Before rolling truffles into a cocoa powder, chill for about 5 minutes.
- Finish with a drizzle with melted chocolate.
- These delicious truffles can be stored in an air-tight container for up to 10 days to a month in the refrigerator.

Low Carb Thin Mint Macaroon Cookies

Serves: 24 / Preparation time: 10 minutes / Cooking time: 16 minutes

1/2 cup granulated sweetener

1 oz. 90% or greater cacao dark chocolate

2 cups desiccated unsweetened coconut

1/4 teaspoon xanthan gum

1/2 cup unsweetened almond milk

3 egg whites

1 1/2 teaspoons peppermint extract

- First, preheat your oven to 325°F (162°C).
- Mix together 1 1/2 teaspoons peppermint extract, 1/2 cup granulated sweetener, 1/2 cup almond milk, and 2 cups coconut in a medium-sized bowl.
- Take another bowl and whisk together 1/4 teaspoon xanthan gum and 3 egg whites until soft peaks form.
- Start folding the egg mixture into the coconut mixture until incorporated.
- Drop the dough mixture into 24 mounds onto a cookie sheet lined with parchment paper using a tablespoon or scoop.
- Flatten each mound into a disk using a spatula.
- Bake until slightly firm, for about 16 minutes. Once done, remove them from the oven and let them cool.
- Add chocolate to a ziplock bag and heat for 30 seconds in a microwave.
- Snip the corner off the bag and squeeze the bag to drop chocolate onto cookies in any pattern.
- Cool and enjoy!

Pumpkin Spice Haystack Cookies

Serves: 12 / Preparation time: 15 minutes / Cooking time: 0 minutes

1 teaspoon ground cinnamon

12 pecans halves to garnish (optional)

4 oz. (1 stick) butter softened

1/4 cup pecans, chopped (optional)

4 oz. cream cheese softened

1 1/2 cups unsweetened coconut, shredded

1/4 cup solid pack pumpkin puree

Pinch of salt

1/3 cup powdered erythritol sweetener

1/8 teaspoon ground nutmeg

1/2 teaspoon unsweetened pure vanilla extract

1/8 teaspoon ground ginger

- Add all the ingredients to a medium-sized bowl except for pecan halves and mix well.
- Scoop dough into 12 mounds using cookie scoop and place on a parchment-lined small platter or cookie sheet.
- Top each cookie with pecan halves and chill until ready to serve.
- These tasty pumpkin spice haystack cookies can be stored in an air-tight container for up to one week in the refrigerator.

Pistachio Truffles

Serves: 10 / Preparation time: 20 minutes / Cooking time: 0 minutes

1/4 teaspoon pure vanilla extract

1/4 cup pistachios, chopped

8 oz. (1 cup) mascarpone cheese, softened

3 tablespoons confectioners style erythritol sweetener

- Combine together 1/4 teaspoon pure vanilla extract, 3 tablespoons erythritol sweetener, and 8 oz. mascarpone cheese in a small-sized bowl.
- Mix with a spatula or fork gently until smooth and well blended.
- Roll into 10 balls using hands (each 1 inch in diameter).
- If it seems too much soft, chill for 10 to 15 minutes and try rolling again.
- Add pistachios to a plate and spread around.
- Roll truffles in pistachios until coated on all sides.
- Chill for half an hour.
- Fat bombs can be stored in an air-tight container for up to 1 week in the refrigerator.

Pistachio Pudding Pie

Serves: 12 / Preparation time: 30 minutes / Cooking time: 12 minutes

For The Pie Crust:

1 batch cookie dough keto pistachio shortbread

For The Filling And Garnish:

3 tablespoons pistachios, chopped (for garnish)

8 oz. mascarpone cheese

2 packages sugar-free pistachio pudding mix

1/2 teaspoon vanilla extract

1.5 cups heavy whipping cream

2 tablespoons confectioners style powdered erythritol

1.5 cups unsweetened almond milk

For The Crust:

- First, preheat your oven to a temperature of 350°F (176°C).
- Press pistachio shortbread cookie dough along the sides and bottom of a pie plate (standard size). Bake for 12 minutes.
- Once done, remove and let it cool.

For The Filling And Garnish:

- Combine together 1.5 cups almond milk, 1/2 cup heavy whipping cream, 8 oz. mascarpone cheese, and 2 packages of pistachio pudding mix. Chill for about 15 minutes.
- In the meantime, mix together the remaining heavy cream, 1/2 teaspoon vanilla extract, and 2 tablespoons powdered erythritol in a separate bowl. Beat well until stiff peaks begin to form, using an electric mixer.
- Now start folding the whipped cream mixture gently into the mixture of pistachio.
- Spoon this mixture into a cooled pie shell, smoothing the top evenly.
- Spoon/pipe remaining whipped cream over top of the pie.
- Finish with a garnishing of chopped pistachios and serve right away!

Strawberry Jello Salad

Serves: 10 / Preparation time: 35 minutes / Cooking time: 0 minutes

1 cup 4% fat large curd cottage cheese

2 cups chopped strawberries + additional for garnish

1 cup heavy whipping cream

1/3 cup unsweetened coconut, shredded

1/2 teaspoon vanilla extract, unsweetened

1/4 cup walnuts, chopped

8 oz. mascarpone cheese, softened

1 box (.6 oz.) sugar-free strawberry jello

- Beat together 1/2 teaspoon vanilla extract and 1 cup heavy whipping cream until stiff peak forms.
- Fold in softened mascarpone cheese until incorporated.
- Stir in 1 box of sugar-free strawberry jello and a cup of cottage cheese.
- Fold in 1/4 cup chopped walnuts, 1/3 cup shredded coconut, and 2 cups chopped strawberries.
- Chill for about 4 hours before serving.
- To unmold, dip the bottom of the container for about 20 seconds in hot water and then flip over a serving platter.
- Finish with a garnish of additional strawberries.
- Keto strawberry jello salad can be stored in an air-tight container for up to 5 days in the refrigerator.

Easy Ice Cream Cake

Serves: 12 / Preparation time: 29 minutes / Cooking time: 14 minutes

For The Chocolate Cookie Crust:

3 tablespoons cocoa powder

1/2 cup granulated erythritol sweetener

6 tablespoons melted butter

2 cups almond flour (superfine blanched)

For The Filling:

2 oz. Lindt 90% chocolate (you can also go for any keto-friendly dark chocolate)

2 pints keto-friendly ice cream of your choice

For The Chocolate Cookie Crust:

- First, preheat your oven to a temperature of 350°F (176°C).
- Mix together all the chocolate cookie crust ingredients in a medium-sized bowl.
- Press this crust into a springform pan (10 inches) firmly and evenly, going up the sides of the curst by about 1/2 inch.
- Bake in a preheated oven for 14 minutes. Once done, remove and let it cool.

To Assemble The Ice Cream Cake:

- Take the ice cream out of the freezer and let it stand until softened.
- Spread crust with melted ice cream using a spatula until smooth. Freeze for half an hour.
- Heat chocolate in the microwave for a minute, remove, and stir well. If not melted, continue heating for another 10 seconds.
- Once melted, let it cool for a few minutes and then add to a plastic baggie, snipping off the bottom tip.
- Take the cake out of the freezer and drizzle with melted chocolate from the bag in your desired pattern.
- Transfer back to the freezer for an hour before slicing.
- Wow! Delicious keto Mediterranean ice cream cake is ready to serve!

Butter Rum Blondies

Serves: 9 / Preparation time: 28 minutes / Cooking time: 20 minutes

1 large egg

1/3 cup walnuts or pecans, chopped

1/2 cup butter, melted

1 tablespoon psyllium husk powder

1/2 cup brown sugar alternative

2 cups superfine blanched almond flour

1/2 teaspoon baking powder

1 teaspoon rum extract

1/4 teaspoon kosher salt

1 teaspoon vanilla extract

- Preheat your oven to 375°F (190°C).
- Add all the ingredients to a large bowl except for nuts. Mix well until combined. Make sure to not over mix; otherwise, it will become tough.
- Stir in 1/3 cup chopped walnuts or pecans.
- Line a square pan (9 x 9) with parchment paper and spoon batter into this pan.
- Spread the top evenly to the edges.
- Bake for 20 minutes.
- Once done, remove and let it cool.
- Slice and serve immediately.
- Keto butter rum blondies can be stored in an air-tight container for more than one week in the refrigerator.

Espresso Chocolate Cheesecake Bars

Serves: 16 / Preparation time: 45 minutes / Cooking time: 33 minutes

For The Chocolate Crust:

2 cups superfine, blanched almond flour

1/3 cup granulated erythritol sweetener

7 tablespoons butter, melted

3 tablespoons cocoa powder

For The Cheesecake:

1 teaspoon vanilla extract

16 oz. full fat cream cheese

2 tablespoons instant espresso powder

2 large eggs

1/2 cup granulated erythritol sweetener

Additional cocoa powder for dusting

- For the chocolate crust: First, preheat your oven to a temperature of 350° F (176°C).

- Mix together all the chocolate crust ingredients in a medium-sized bowl and transfer to a parchment-lined pan (9 x 9), pressing it firmly into the bottom.

- Bake for 8 minutes. Once done, remove and let it cool.

    For The Cheesecake Filling:

- For the cheesecake filling: Add all the filling ingredients to the blender and blend well until smooth.

- Pour this mixture over the baked crust, spreading the top evenly with a spatula.

- Bake cheesecake bars for 25 minutes or until set.

- Once done, remove cheesecake bars from the oven and let them cool.

- Dust with cocoa powder and chill for an hour.

- Cut into four rows of squares to serve.

- These chocolate cheesecake bars can be stored in an air-tight container for up to 5 days in the refrigerator.

Thumbprint Cookies

Serves: 10 / Preparation time: 10 minutes / Cooking time: 18 minutes

5 tablespoons sugar-free strawberry preserves

1 large egg, beaten

1/3 cup walnuts, finely chopped

1/2 cup salted butter, softened

1/2 teaspoon baking powder

1 teaspoon vanilla extract

2 cups superfine blanched almond flour

2/3 cup powdered erythritol sweetener

Pinch of kosher salt

- First, preheat your oven to 375° F (190°C).
- Mix together all the ingredients in a medium-sized bowl except for walnuts and strawberry preserves.
- Once you have the dough, form it into 1.5 inch balls.
- Roll these balls in the walnuts until coated on all sides.
- Line a cookie sheet with parchment paper and place cookies onto it.
- Bake for 8 minutes.
- Once done, take it out from the oven and press a small dent into the center of each.
- Place a teaspoon of jam in each dent and continue baking for another 10 minutes.
- Remove cookies to a platter carefully, and cool them before serving.

Keto Mixed Berry Slab Pie

Serves: 12 / Preparation time: 10 minutes / Cooking time: 40 minutes

For The Crust:

2 tablespoons psyllium husk powder

2 tablespoons granulated sweetener

1/2 cup butter, melted

1/8 teaspoon salt

2 1/2 cups superfine blanched almond flour

For The Filling:

1/2 cup granulated sweetener

1 teaspoon vanilla extract

5 cups mixed berries

1 teaspoon ground cinnamon

- Preheat your oven to 350° F (176°C).
- Add all the crust ingredients to a medium-sized bowl and mix well.
- Remove about 1/3 of the dough (1 1/4 cups) from the bowl for the top crust.
- Press the remaining dough into a baking sheet (13 x 9).
- Bake until light golden brown for 6 to 8 minutes.
- Add all the filling ingredients to a bowl and stir well until combined.
- Spread berry onto the baked crust evenly.
- Top with remaining crust either rolled and cut into strips lattice style or crumbled over Dutch style.
- Bake for 30 to 32 minutes on top oven rack. The top must be golden brown.
- Once done, take it out from the oven and leave for 15 minutes until cooled.
- Cut into 12 even squares.
- It can be stored in an air-tight container for up to a week in the refrigerator.

Coconut Shortbread Cookies

Serves: 16 cookies / Preparation time: 22 minutes / Cooking time: 15 minutes

1/2 cup confectioners style powdered erythritol

1/3 cup unsweetened coconut, finely shredded

6 tablespoons butter, melted

1 teaspoon coconut extract

2 cups superfine blanched almond flour

- Mix together all the ingredients in a large-sized bowl except for coconut until fully combined.
- Form a tightly packed log of dough with your hands (about 8-inch long).
- Wrap dough in a plastic wrap and squeeze it tightly,
- Unroll the dough carefully, sprinkle with shredded coconut, and then roll to coat the dough completely.
- Again wrap in plastic, twisting the two ends.
- Place in the freezer for half an hour.
- Unwrap the dough carefully and cut ½ inch thick discs.
- Place discs onto a cookie sheet lined with parchment paper and cook for 12 to 15 minutes at 350°F (176°C) or until golden brown.
- Once done, remove and let the discs cool completely.
- These cookies can be stored in an air-tight container for up to 5 days to 6 months in the freezer.

Pistachio Fudge

Serves: 7 / Preparation time: 12 minutes / Cooking time: 0 minutes

1/2 teaspoon vanilla extract

1/2 cup pistachios, roughly chopped

1 cup cacao butter wafers

1/2 teaspoon psyllium husk powder

1/2 cup mascarpone cheese

2 –3 drops green food coloring

2 tablespoons butter

1/2 cup powdered erythritol

1/4 teaspoon almond extract

Pinch of salt

- Add cocoa butter pieces to a microwave-safe bowl and heat for 2 minutes on high.
- Stir in 1/4 teaspoon almond extract, 1/2 cup mascarpone cheese, 1/2 teaspoon vanilla extract, 1/2 cup powdered erythritol, pinch of salt, and 2 tablespoons butter, until smooth.
- Whisk in 1/2 teaspoon psyllium husk powder, and 2 to 3 drops of green food coloring, until well blended.
- Stir in 1/2 cup roughly chopped pistachios.
- Place into a parchment-lined loaf pan for a thicker fudge or a parchment-lined baking sheet for a thinner bark.
- Chill until firm and set.
- Break or slices into 12 equal portions.
- Pistachio fudge can be stored in an air-tight container for up to 2 weeks in the refrigerator or up to 6 months.

Easy Low Carb Mug Cake

Serves: 1 / Preparation time: 5 minutes / Cooking time: 2 minutes

Pinch of salt

1 teaspoon sugar-free chocolate chips

3 tablespoons coconut flour

1/2 teaspoon vanilla extract

2 tablespoon unsweetened cocoa powder

1 egg yolk

2 1/2 tablespoons monk fruit sweetener

1 tablespoon coconut oil, melted

1/2 teaspoon baking powder

5 tablespoons unsweetened vanilla almond milk

- Add all the dry ingredients to a bowl and mix well.
- In a separate bowl, whisk together leftover ingredients except for chocolate chips.
- Fold this mixture into dry ingredients until smooth.
- Next, stir in chocolate chips.
- Transfer to a 14-16 oz. Mug and spread the top evenly.
- Cook for 2 and a half minutes in a 1000-watt microwave, or until the top is set.

Sugar-Free Low Carb Pecan Pie

Serves: 12 / Preparation time: 10 minutes / Cooking time: 15 minutes

1 1/2 cups pecans

1 teaspoon maple extract

1 almond flour pie crust

1 teaspoon vanilla

2/3 cup powdered erythritol sweetener

3/4 teaspoon salt

6 tablespoons unsalted butter

2 large eggs

1 1/4 cups heavy whipping cream

- Set a high-sided frying pan over medium-low flame. Add in 6 tablespoons unsalted butter and 2/3 cup powdered erythritol sweetener and whisk well for 5-7 minutes or until mixture is golden brown.
- Once golden, whisk in 1 1/4 cups heavy whipping cream and bring to a light simmer.
- Cook for about 8 minutes until the mixture just begins to thicken, stirring frequently. Once done, remove from heat and allow to cool for half an hour.
- Once cooled enough, heat your oven to a temperature of 350 degrees F (176.667°C).
- Spread 1 1/2 cups of pecans on a large baking sheet and bake until toasted and golden brown. It may take 10 to 12 minutes.
- Once done, remove them and roughly chop.
- Add eggs to a cool mixture along with 3/4 teaspoon salt, 1 teaspoon maple extract, and 1 teaspoon vanilla. Whisk well until everything is smooth.
- Stir in toasted and roughly chopped pecans.
- Pour this filling over cooled pie crust and bake for half an hour or until the top is set.
- Once done, let it cool and then refrigerate overnight.
- The next day, cut into slices and enjoy!

Chocolate Cake

Serves: 24 / Preparation time: 10 minutes / Cooking time: 30 minutes

3/4 teaspoon salt	2/3 cup cocoa powder, sifted
1 batch keto chocolate frosting	1/2 cup avocado oil
2 cups almond flour	1/4 cup coconut flour
1/2 cup boiling water	4 large eggs, at room temperature
1 cup swerve sweetener	2 teaspoons baking powder
2 teaspoons vanilla	1 teaspoon baking soda

- Preheat your oven to 350°F (176°C).
- Take two cake pans (9-inch each) and line bottoms with parchment paper.
- Grease the sides of pans with oil.
- Combine together all the dry ingredients in a bowl.
- Add in 1/2 cup avocado oil, 4 eggs, and 2 teaspoons vanilla. Whisk well until combined.
- Pour half a cup of boiling water and continue whisking until well-combined.
- Divide this batter among the prepared pans and cook for half an hour, or until a tester inserted comes out clean from the center.
- Cool and enjoy!

Low Carb Pumpkin Cheesecake

Serves: 12 / Preparation time: 1 hour 10 minutes / Cooking time: 1 hour 10 minutes

2/3 cup canned pumpkin

1 tablespoon pumpkin pie spice

1 gluten-free cracker crust, baked

1 tablespoon vanilla extract

16 oz. (2 blocks) full fat cream cheese, at room temperature

2 large eggs, at room temp

3/4 cup monk fruit

- Preheat the oven to 325 °F (162°C).
- Beat together 3/4 cup monk fruit and 16 oz. Full fat cream cheese until smooth, using an electric hand mixer, scraping down the sides in between.
- Add leftover ingredients and beat until just combined. Do not overbeat; otherwise, too much air will be developed in the cheesecake.
- Take graham cracker crust out of the freezer and wrap its bottom and up the sides with a few layers of tin foil tightly.
- Place pan inside a large roasting pan.
- Pour cheesecake batter onto graham cracker crust and smooth the top evenly with a spatula.
- Place in the middle oven rack and fill the roasting pan with water in a way that it comes halfway up to the pan.
- Bake for about 55 to 60 minutes, or until completely cooked through. Turn off your oven, cracking its door slightly.
- Let your cake sit inside the oven for about 15 minutes. Then let it cool completely.
- Once cooled, refrigerate for at least 8 hours or overnight, covered.
- Run a sharp knife along the sides after taking it out of the refrigerator. Remove to a platter and slice and serve!

Low Carb Sugar-Free Blueberry Muffins

Serves: 12 / Preparation time: 20 minutes / Cooking time: 25 minutes

3/4 cup monk fruit

2/3 cup fresh blueberries,

3 cups almond flour

2 teaspoons vanilla extract

4 tablespoons coconut flour, packed

1/2 cup unsweetened applesauce

1 tablespoon baking powder

3 large eggs, at room temperature

1 teaspoon sea salt

7 tablespoons coconut oil, melted

1 teaspoon baking soda

- Preheat the oven to 350°F (176°C).
- Grease a muffin pan with oil spray.
- Mix together 4 tablespoons coconut flour, 1 teaspoon baking soda, 3 cups almond flour, 1 tablespoon baking powder, and 1 teaspoon sea salt.
- In a separate bowl, beat together 3/4 cup monk fruit, 3 large eggs, 7 tablespoons coconut oil, 1/2 cup unsweetened applesauce, and 2 teaspoons vanilla extract using an electric hand mixer.
- Stir 2/3 cup fresh blueberries in almond flour mixture until combined. Leave the batter for 5-10 minutes.
- Divide among 12 muffin cavities and bake for about 24 to 25 minutes until a tester inserted comes out clean from the center.
- Once done, let them cool, and then run a sharp knife around the edges to lose each muffin.
- Enjoy delicious low-carb, sugar-free blueberry muffins.

Lemon Ice Cream

Serves: 6 / Preparation time: 1 hour 30 minutes / Cooking time: 0 minutes

3 large eggs

1¾ cups heavy whipping cream

1 lemon, zest, and juice

1/3 cup (2½ oz.) erythritol

2-3 yellow food color drops

- In a small-sized bowl, beat egg whites until stiff.
- Take another bowl and whisk together 1/3 cup erythritol and egg yolks until fluffy.
- Add in drops of food color, lemon juice, and zest.
- Fold egg whites into a yolk mixture carefully.
- Add 1¾ cups heavy whipping cream to a large-sized bowl and whip until soft peaks form.
- Gently start folding the egg mixture into whipped cream.
- Pour this batter into an ice cream maker and freeze as per the manufacturer's directions. Alternatively, place a batter bowl in the freezer for 2 hours, stirring every half an hour.
- If frozen, leave it for 15 minutes at room temperature before serving.

Made in the USA
Monee, IL
10 June 2023